Rushing Waters
Rising Dreams

Rushing Waters
Rising Dreams

How the Arts are
Transforming a Community

EDITED BY
DENISE M. SANDOVAL, PH.D.
LUIS J. RODRIGUEZ

Tia Chucha Press
Los Angeles

Harry!
Thank you for
always inspiring me as
an Artist and a FRIEND!
I hope you enjoy the Book!

Denise Sandoval

Pages 64-65: Excerpts are reprinted with permission from the publisher of "I Am Rene, the Boy" and "Rene has Two Last Names" by René Colato Laínez (©2005 and 2009 Arte Público Press—University of Houston).

Page 14, photo: Pacoima Flood, February 1978. Robert Franklin (photographer). Robert Franklin Papers, Special Collections and Archives. Reprinted with permission of Oviatt Library, California State University, Northridge.

Printed in the United States.

ISBN 978-1-882688-43-2

Book Design: Jane Brunette
Cover images by Giovanni Darkins, Javier Martinez, Estevan Oriol, Rick Ortega, Luz Rodriguez, and Violet Soto.

Published by:

Tia Chucha Press
A Project of Tia Chucha's Centro Cultural, Inc.
PO Box 328
San Fernando, CA 91341
www.tiachucha.com

Distributed by:

Northwestern University Press
Chicago Distribution Center
11030 South Langley Avenue
Chicago IL 60628

Tia Chucha Press is the publishing wing of Tia Chucha's Centro Cultural, Inc., a 501 (c) (3) nonprofit corporation. Tia Chucha's Centro Cultural has received funding for this book from the Los Angeles County Arts Commission, the National Endowment for the Arts, and individual donors. Other funding for Tia Chucha's Centro Cultural's programming and operations has come from the California Arts Council, Los Angeles County Arts Commission, Los Angeles Department of Cultural Affairs, The California Community Foundation, the Annenberg Foundation, the Weingart Foundation, National Association of Latino Arts and Culture, Ford Foundation, MetLife, Southwest Airlines, the Andy Warhol Foundation for the Visual Arts, the Thrill Hill Foundation, the Middleton Foundation, Center for Cultural Innovation, John Irvine Foundation, Not Just Us Foundation, the Attias Family Foundation, and the Guacamole Fund, among others. Donations have also come from Bruce Springsteen, John Densmore of The Doors, Jackson Browne, Lou Adler, Richard Foos, Gary Stewart, Charles Wright, Adrienne Rich, Tom Hayden, Dave Marsh, Jack Kornfield, Jesus Trevino, David Sandoval, Denise Chávez and John Randall of the Border Book Festival, Luis & Trini Rodríguez, and many more.

DEDICATIONS

LUIS RODRIGUEZ:

To

Tony Hernandez
Tia Chucha patron and helper, best friend, Mayan cholo of Guatemalan/Mexican descent,
and Xicano through and through

Jeffrey Guido De Rienzo
Friend, organizer, revolutionary, and writer

Piri Thomas
Flowmaster, Boricua carnal, spiritual mentor to my poetry and prose

And

Maria de Jesus Rodriguez
"Tia Chucha"

.....

DENISE M. SANDOVAL, PH.D.:

To

Dr. Rodolfo F. Acuña
Mentor, Teacher, Activist, Friend, and "Godfather" of Chicana/o Studies

Young Warriors
The next generation of artists, writers, activists, leaders, teachers, and scholars,
especially Mayra Zaragoza, Violet Soto, Karina Ceja, and Angel Hernandez
—the future of community activism looks bright and firme in their hands.

Photo: Violet Soto

Table of Contents

Photo: Javier Martinez

Art is on the side of the oppressed.
Think before you shudder at the simplistic dictum
and its heretical definition of the freedom of art.
For if art is freedom of the spirit,
how can it exist in the oppressors?

EDITH WHARTON

The Vitality of the Arts

Mural: Danny Trejo. Artist: Levi Ponce. Pacoima, CA. Photo: Javier Martinez

BY LUIS J. RODRIGUEZ

THE BOOK in your hands is about a particular place and a particular time. The place is the Northeast San Fernando Valley, an often forgotten section of Los Angeles snuggled away between the more developed West San Fernando Valley and bedroom communities like Valencia, Flintridge/La Canada, and nearby Pasadena. This area holds around half a million people, the second largest community of Mexicans and Central Americans in the country after East Los Angeles. It includes one of the poorest neighborhoods, Pacoima, with gangs, housing projects, struggling families, next to other working class enclaves such as Sylmar, San Fernando (a separate two-and-half-square mile city), Arleta, and Sunland-Tujunga.

The time is more or less from 1990 to 2010. Twenty years of arts development, expressions, and potential. It's also about an institution, small but crucial, called Tia Chucha's Centro Cultural—a bookstore, performance space, art gallery, arts/music/dance/theater/writers workshop center, Internet Café, and publishing house. Until Tia Chucha's opened its doors as a cultural café in December of 2001, there were no trade bookstores, no movie houses, no art galleries, or multi-arts cultural spaces in the Northeast San Fernando Valley (and despite being situated in the "Entertainment Capital of the World").

This book, however, is also about every community, every poor and deprived working class area in the United States, especially during one of the most destabilizing and persistent economic crises. The Northeast San Fernando Valley used to have a thriving auto plant, a brass foundry, aerospace shops, and warehouses. By 2000 most of these jobs had vanished as de-industrialization gripped the whole country beginning in the mid-1970s. People often forget that the Los Angeles area has been the country's largest manufacturing center (or they think Hollywood is the *only* industry). L.A. was home to all major industries, including the largest mainland port (Los Angeles/Long Beach) as well as steel mills, stockyards, garment industries, refineries, and canneries. Although not in the Midwest (with blue-collar cities like Chicago, Detroit, and Pittsburgh), Los Angeles suffered like the "Rust Belt."

With de-industrialization came more street violence: The L.A. area already had some of the oldest and violent gangs among its massive Chicano/Mexicano populations (the earliest began in the late 1800s to early 1900s and continue to the present), with newer gangs such as Crips and Bloods among African Americans (from the early 1970s), and more recent gangs (from the 1980s till today) like the Mara Salvatrucha from among Salvadoran and other Central American refugees. Crack cocaine first made its appearance in L.A. in the early 1980s (quickly spreading to other urban core communities), followed by "chronic," "crank," more powerful heroin, stronger inhalants, "ecstasy," prescriptions drugs, and more. By the early 2000s, these kinds of illicit drugs became the norm around the country.

From 1980 to the year 2000, street gangs became larger, more entrenched in the drug trade, which had become a viable economic activity in the wake of the industrial jobs loss. An estimated 15,000 young people in the L.A. area were killed in the ensuing street wars during those years. And there was accompanying police repression. In twenty years, the City of Los Angeles instituted around forty gang injunctions against local street associations, including the second largest in California—nine-and-a-half square miles that encompassed much of Sylmar, San Fernando, and Pacoima.

San Fernando Valley/818 Pride. Anthony Hernandez, Tattoo Artist, Sylmar, CA. Photo: Estevan Oriol

Calavera Familia. Dia de Los Muertos Festival 2011. San Fernando, CA. Photo: Javier Martinez

out" laws, trying juveniles as adults, and enhanced sentencing for suspected gang involvement, among other new laws, became the norm. By 2010, California had the largest state prison system, going from fifteen prisons in the early 1970s to around thirty-five. All this impacted the Northeast San Fernando Valley.

Yet at the start of a new century, the exponential growth of the digital age including the Internet, among other technologies, opened up a re-imagining and re-shaping of everything—from the economy, to schools, to household structures, to the workplace, to personal and social relationships. We continue to stand on the threshold of another time, a new epoch, igniting wondrous ideas and new forms of discourse, business, and governance.

Gang injunctions outlawed the gathering of more than two suspected gang members in public areas as well as baseball bats and cell phones during certain hours, and strict curfews, wanton police stops, and the gathering of photos/names for a gang database—impositions that many dictatorial third world countries wouldn't do. Such efforts, including increased gentrification, forced many poor families, almost all black and brown, to be squeezed out of their communities. One outcome was that L.A.-based gangs became the fastest growing trend around the country. By the mid-1990s, mass deportations of jail and prison convicts flooded countries like Mexico, El Salvador, Guatemala, Honduras, Belize, Armenia, and Cambodia with tens of thousands of L.A.-based gang members. The gangs, instead of dying out, became more decentralized and sophisticated.

During this same period, "three strikes and you're

THE AIM OF THIS BOOK is to help a whole culture find the unity-in-diversity, the commonalities among the differences, the connective tissue between our varied and seemingly disparate lives. Our long-range objectives in the coming period should be for the integrated growth of the arts, morals (the proper and respectful relations with each other, the Earth, and spirit) as well as science.

As many philosophers have stated before—for Beauty, Good, and Truth.

This book, therefore, could have been situated in Flint, Michigan; Laredo, Texas; Paterson, New Jersey; Grants, New Mexico; Portland, Oregon; Atlanta, Georgia—it just happens to be the Northeast San Fernando Valley.

My wife Trini grew up in the Pacoima barrio. For generations migrants had been coming here to toil in the fields as well as the incipient industry, mostly from Mexico, but also significant numbers of African Americans, whites, and later Central Americans and Asians. In the 1970s, African Americans were actually the majority. The name Pacoima means "rushing waters" in the Tataviam native language. Yet despite the poverty and crime surrounding them, Trini's family of eleven siblings, whose parents were hard-working, barely educated migrants from Jalisco, Mexico, never got into gangs or drugs—they became known for having survived against the odds.

Although Trini left the area for some twenty-five years, including seventeen years in Chicago, upon her return in the year 2000 she saw how culturally deprived the Northeast Valley had become.

In fact, the country as a whole appeared to be in a particularly dark period. By 2012, everything was in the throes of crisis (politics, finances, culture, religion, family, and more). Funds for the arts were being cut out of schools, from government programs, and in many foundations. And few people, especially among our elected leaders, corporations, spiritual guides, and academics, had truly holistic and unifying answers.

What a time to live, to dream, to create.

THE STORY OF ARTS DEVELOPMENT in the Northeast San Fernando Valley is also about the vitality of the arts in every neighborhood. I contend we need national and local neighborhood arts policies more than ever—where independent bookstores, media centers, Internet cafes, uniquely rich coffee houses, open mics, public art projects, storefront cultural spaces, art galleries, writing centers, theaters, and more can thrive, exhibiting the local flavor of each place, instead of the concentration of the arts in pricey museums, downtown arts corridors, or tourist havens.

To end, here is the statement I wrote for the trailer we used to raise funds in 2011 for this book and film about how the arts transforms communities. It makes the case for why we need places like Tia Chucha's, why we need fully developed community-based arts education, expression, production, and exhibition everywhere, anytime:

The first move from chaos isn't order—it's creativity. In murals, music, theater, cafés, and poetry. It comes from within people, within families, within community. It rises from the hunger people have for knowledge, ideas, and stories.

In the neglected Northeast San Fernando Valley, many can only see chaos. We knew that several companies—including bookstores—had been asked to set up shop here. We heard they wouldn't touch this area with a ten-foot pole. What they failed to recognize was that poor people, those with little material means, have an abundance of imagination and talents. We found art, song, music, poetry, and more already existing among members of this community. As the saying goes, "artists are not a special kind of people; everyone is a special kind of artist." We have many passions, attributes and capacities the day we're born—they are part of our destinies, our callings, imprinted in our souls. The arts have consistently proven to be the most effective means

The story of arts development in the Northeast San Fernando Valley is also about the vitality of the arts in every neighborhood.

to lift the most desolate areas, bring together fractured communities, and transform lives, especially those in the grips of violence. Through dance, theater, media, writing, and music, whole communities, in particular youth, connect to the inexhaustible possibilities that exist in their immense capacity to be creative.

The worst aspect of poverty is the spiritual poverty that accompanies it. When we provide places for people to imagine, to dialogue, to express, to share, and to create, we uplift the spirit needed to also help remove the real constraints of current economic and social realities. This is truly substantive soul work. We have survived and succeeded because we have always responded to obstacles by becoming more imaginative and encompassing. We have refused to give up on the arts. We have refused to give up on artists and, as we are all artists, we have refused to give up on our community. The first move from chaos isn't order—it's creativity. And given the means, there is no limit to what this community can create.

¡La Lucha Continua!

Why Community History Matters

The Role of the Arts
and the Struggle for
Space and Place
in the Northeast
San Fernando Valley.

By Denise M. Sandoval, Ph.D.

"Without a sense of community, a sense of history as a community, people become vulnerable to the plans and whims of dominant groups, which can not only displace them, but control them in other ways as well."
— *Rodolfo F. Acuña*

IF ONE WERE TO RELY on popular images of the Northeast San Fernando Valley, Pacoima was put on the map by the movie *La Bamba* (1987), the story of native son and young rock & roll singer Ritchie Valens, who died tragically in a plane crash in 1959 at the age of seventeen as his star was rising. Ritchie Valens is the Guardian Angel of "Pacas"—the locals' name for this barrio. His image is immortalized in Pacoima and can be found in various murals; he even has a park and recreation center named after him. San Fernando on the other hand, is known as the "First City of the Valley" since in 1874 it became the valley's first organized community. It is also known as "The Mission City" because of its close proximity to the San Fernando Mission (established in 1797), which is located in Mission Hills. Finally, Sylmar, lying at the base of the beautiful San Gabriel Mountains, became part of Los Angeles earthquake history when in February 9, 1971 this community was the center of a 6.6 magnitude earthquake. These popular images and notable facts often obscure the voices and stories of the people who live in those communities, which speaks to the history of struggle for "space" and "place" in regards to not only cultural identity[-ies], but community survival.

Community histories explore individuals and communities as the focus of history and allow for different voices to be heard across generations, regions, race/ethnicity, class, gender and sexual orientation. Community histories are important tools in writing history since they challenge dominant methods in the discipline of history where the historian is an "objective" storyteller, usually an "outsider" of that community, and uses documents and events to tell "their story." In collecting the essays, poems, interviews and photos for the book *Rushing Waters, Rising Dreams*, Luis J. Rodriguez and I had many conversations about allowing these communities to tell their stories about growing up in the Northeast San Fernando Valley, as well as reflect the transformative power of the arts in sustaining those communities over these last twenty years.

This is the first book on the role of cultural arts that places the focus on the Northeast San Fernando Valley and allows the people of those communities to speak their stories—their truths. There are many books that document the history of the San Fernando Valley, but many of them focus on the West side of the Valley, the more affluent and well known side, areas like Northridge, Encino, and Sherman Oaks. There are also many books on Chicano/Latino history in Los Angeles (heavily focused on East Los Angeles/Boyle Heights, which is understandable given the early roots of the city of Los Angeles). But what is missing are the histories of the Chicano/Mexican/Latino communities in the Northeast San Fernando Valley—which is about a thirty minute drive, barring traffic, from downtown Los Angeles. This book is not the definitive book on those missing histories, but it is an attempt to contribute a more holistic and complex picture of Los Angeles history, San Fernando Valley history, as well as multicultural U.S. history using "the people's voices."

I came to this project as a cultural historian. I am a professor of Chicana/o Studies at California State University, Northridge (CSUN) since 2002, and it was my friendship and admiration of the work of Luis, his wife Trini Rodriguez, and the people I met at Tia Chucha's

This is the first book on the role of cultural arts that places the focus on the Northeast San Fernando Valley and allows the people of those communities to speak their stories— their truths.

that brought me to this project. CSUN is the main four-year university that services the entire San Fernando Valley, and the majority of our students are from this area. In particular, many of the Chicano/Latino students in my classes are from the communities of Pacoima, Sylmar and San Fernando. Yet, in the process of organizing this book, I was reminded of my deeper connection to the Northeast San Fernando Valley—my deep commitment to Chicana/o Studies and Ethnic Studies as a discipline and as a tool for social justice.

There was a hunger growing inside of me for filling in the gaps of my education, one where I never learned about Mexican American history and culture.

When I was an undergraduate at UC Berkeley in the early 1990s, I decided to major in Ethnic Studies once I experienced my first Chicano Studies class. There was a hunger growing inside of me for filling in the gaps of my education, one where I never learned about Mexican American history and culture, the histories of people of color, and feminist perspectives to understanding our world. For the first time, I began to understand my personal history as a second generation Mexican American young woman in Los Angeles in a critical and self-reflective manner. I chose Ethnic Studies/Chicano Studies because it was a discipline that was born out of the civil rights movements of the 1960s and 1970s and it was committed to linking its scholarship to "the community"(-ies), especially those that are economically and politically disempowered. I absorbed all the teachings at UC Berkeley—"Be the Change You Want in the World," "Power to the People," and "The Personal as Political"—and I realized at the age of 22 that I wanted to write books about Chicana/o History. I also wanted to work in the area of Ethnic Studies/Chicano Studies. More importantly I wanted to connect my work at the university level to the community. When I graduated from Berkeley, I defined myself as "Chicana." In 1993,

I arrived on the CSUN campus to pursue a Masters of Arts in Chicana and Chicano Studies and my relationship to the San Fernando Valley began.

THE 1990S WERE an important time period for Chicanos/Latinos as well as many people of color in Los Angeles. One seminal event that occurred on March 3, 1991 in Lakeview Terrace, a couple of miles from the present Tia Chucha's, was the beating of Rodney King by the Los Angeles Police Department. This event captured on video the tensions that had previously existed between many communities of color and the police department.

When the police officers were acquitted one year later, the Los Angeles Riots/Rebellion erupted on April 29, 1992. This rebellion was about more than police brutality—it revealed the historical and continued effects of racism and social inequalities on Black and Brown communities. Many people described this eruption as "The Watts Riots" (1965) for the post-Civil Rights generation. The 1990s kicked off with a fiery explosion for the people of Los Angeles. As the demographics shifted in California (or the "Browning of California" as some have called it), the rise in nativist and racist attacks toward the Latino community was the result. For instance, California legislation such as Proposition 187 (1994) denied health and educational services to undocumented people; Proposition 209 (1996) effectively put an end to affirmative action programs; and Proposition 227 (1998) eliminated bilingual education in public schools.

By the 2000 Census, half of the nation's Latinos lived in California or Texas. According to Rodolfo F. Acuña, "The U.S. Mexican population grew by 53 percent, with registered voters increasing from 5.5 million in 1994 to 8 million in 2000" (pg. 395). The report by Valley Communities in 2004 revealed how Latinos were the majority in the Northeast San Fernando Valley (72.0 percent)—and the percentage of Latinos in the city of San Fernando was 91.4 percent; Pacoima 88.8 percent; and Sylmar 75.1 percent. This meant that over the last twenty years, Chicanos/Latinos continued to be an important political and demographic presence. At the same time during this time period, Los Angeles experienced a flowering of Chicano art. A new generation of Chicano activists and artists came of age in the 1990s as our communities were under attack; they staked their claim on the Los Angeles landscape as a space to create empowerment and change. From East Los Angeles to South Los Angeles to the Northeast San Fernando Valley, artists and writers used art to tell their history and mobilize people to action, especially around issues of social justice. Writers in particular made an impact on both the local and national level by documenting life in the Northeast San Fernando Valley.

THE YEAR 1993 in particular proved to be an important one for the Northeast San Fernando Valley. Mary Helen Ponce published her book "Hoyt Street" which was her autobiography of growing up in Pacoima in the 1940s and it vividly captures the life and people of this community. Ponce herself admits her book began as an anthropological project and she views it as "community history." Her story documents the struggles of being Mexican American during this time period and emphasizes the roles of family and neighborhood in shaping one's cultural identity. She writes:

> People in Pacoima, I often thought, needed more space than did those in upwardly mobile San Fernando, where homes had sidewalks and paved streets, but sat close together, as if afraid to breathe too much of their neighbor's air. On Hoyt Street, most residents had once lived in Mexican ranchitos and had a greater need for land. In the large double lots, they planted fruit trees, vegetable and flower gardens, and assorted hierbas that also grew in Mexico. (pg. 7)

Also that same year, Cornerstone Theater Company premiered the historical fantasy play called "Rushing Waters," written by Migdalia Cruz at the Boys and Girls Club of the San Fernando Valley. The play is based on the history of Pacoima and set in a time period after a big earthquake hits Los Angeles and notable figures appear in the play—such as singer and Pacoima native son Ritchie Valens; Joe Louis who had "Joe Louis Homes" named after him, a tract-home development for African American home buyers in Pacoima in the 1940s; and Nancy Avery, the postmaster of Pacoima from 1961 to 1984, the first Black person to hold a major post office position in the United States. The play marked the first time the theater company produced a play from the "ground up" in a multiracial community like Pacoima. They realized the necessity of documenting community histories outside of the well-known areas like East Los Angeles and South Central. The play also celebrates the beauty of the people and neigh-

In the large double lots on Hoyt street, they planted fruit trees, vegetable and flower gardens, and assorted hierbas that also grew in Mexico.

borhood of Pacoima and speaks to the importance of activism to create change. This is evidenced in the chorus led by the characters of Mocapia and Amiocap, the mother and father figures for the children of "Rushing Waters" in the play:

> Put your hands together and say "Ho-oh!"
> Say "Ho-Pacoima!"
> Now say it again "Ho-oh! Ho-Pacoima!"
>
> WELCOME TO A PLACE
> WE ALL MUST REMEMBER—
> A PLACE OF LIFE, LOVE
> AND MULTIRACIAL SPLENDOR.
> A PLACE YOU CAN'T IGNORE
> NOR DEPLORE ANYMORE—
> IT'S A PLACE CALLED "RUSHING WATERS,"
> A PLACE THEY LOVED TO HATE,
> BUT WE'VE CHANGED THE SYSTEM—
> WE'VE CHANGED OUR FATE (pg. 3).

Finally, two other events marked the year 1993 and are relevant to the book *Rushing Waters, Rising Dreams.* Luis J. Rodriguez published his award-winning memoir of gang life, *Always Running: La Vida Loca, Gang Days in L.A.* The book was an important one to not only the Chicano community, but also to the literary community in general, with its honesty and humanity toward a topic that often generated fear in many across the United States. Its timely arrival after the 1992 Riots/Rebellion provided audiences with a space to dialogue and strategize over how to move forward as a city.

As Luis writes in his essay to this book, the 1980s were devastating for many communities of color that were struggling through gang and drug wars. Luis became a spokesperson to the dominant media about the crises plaguing the inner cities, as well as outlining so-

The 1980s were devastating for many communities of color that were struggling through gang and drug wars.

lutions. His work as a writer and activist has impacted the lives of many, even those living and dealing with similar issues in other parts of the world.

Yet, the book was not without controversy when in 1999 the American Library Association called *Always Running* one of the 100 most censored books in the United States. Luis nonetheless has dedicated his life to the arts and service. As he writes in his essay, "the aim of this book is to help a whole culture find the unity-in-diversity, the commonalities among the differences, the connective tissue between our varied and seemingly disparate lives."

It is the power of the individual and the collective to create transformative change with their lives in service of others that was practiced by the iconic leader of the United Farmworkers of America, César E. Chávez. And on April 23, 1993, when Chávez died in his sleep at the age of 66, a new generation of activists was poised to pick up the torch and carry on the legacy of "Si Se Puede." The Northeast San Fernando Valley was more than ready to answer Chávez's call to action.

BARRIOLOGY

There is a framework for understanding the history of struggle and role of cultural movements in the Northeast San Fernando Valley anchored in barrio life—a "barriology." In *Barrio Logos: Space and Place in Urban Chicano Literature and Culture (2000)*, Raul Villa examines how within Los Angeles, working class struggles and cultural movements of Mexican Americans can be mapped. He labels these cultural moments and struggles "barriology," which is the documentation of the tensions based in "the practice of everyday life" for barrio residents of Los Angeles. Villa further explains the importance of barrio life to cultural space and identity:

> Manifesting alternative needs and interests of those of the dominant public sphere, the expressive practices of barrio social and cultural reproduction—from the mundane exercises of daily round and leisure activities to the formal articulation of community defensive goals in organizational forums and discursive media—reveal multiple possibilities for re-creating and re-imagining dominant urban space as community enabling place. Thus they contribute to a cumulative anti-discipline that subverts the totalizing impulse of the dominant social space containing the barrios. Collectively, these community-sustaining practices constitute a tactical ethos (and aesthetic) of barriology ever engaged in counterpoint to external barrioization (pg. 6).

Villa's definition of barriology is relevant to the documentation of the cultural, artistic, and activist history in the Northeast San Fernando Valley. There are two points made by Villa in the above definition of barriology that are central: 1) the way in which expressive practices of barrio social and cultural reproduction reveal multiple possibilities for "recreating and re-imagining dominant urban space as community enabling space"; and, 2) how these collective moments operate as attempts by barrio residents to create community sustaining practices as a tactical ethos (and aesthetic) of barriology ever engaged in counterpoint to external barrioization.

A beginning point to this barriology history lesson

must begin with the legacy of the Chicana/o Movement and how it shifted definitions of cultural identity, created a new generation of leaders and activists, transformed the barrio into "community enabling place" and used art as a weapon for education, empowerment, and social justice as both a "tactical ethos and aesthetic."

THE LEGACY: THE CHICANA/O MOVEMENT

The Chicana/o Movement (1962-1975) was the political arena in which Chicanos engaged in activism in regards to civil rights. They also developed a collective identity that challenged the status quo of oppression and inequality that many Chicanos experienced in the United States (Chavez, 2002; Acuña, 2000; Garcia, 1997; Marin, 1991; Muñoz, 1989). The term Chicano was a political label adopted by some Mexican Americans. They named themselves on their own terms (instead of having a label placed on them by the dominant culture) and also connected their lives to their indigenous heritage. Chicanos fought in their communities for social change, while embracing the philosophies of self-determination and empowerment. There were a variety of movements occurring through the Southwest, many different leaders and political agendas—yet all are defined under the umbrella label: "The Chicano Movement." The Chicana/o Movement directly influenced much of the work of Chicano artists and community members throughout the barrios of the Southwest.

The most well known movement was led by César E. Chávez and Dolores Huerta and sought to organize a labor union for farm workers in California. In 1962, the National Farm Worker Association (later named the United Farm Workers of America—UFW) led a struggle to end the pervasive poverty and caste-like status of Mexican Americans in the fields. The NFWA advocated for labor contracts between the growers and the workers, and demanded an end to the Bracero Program, which was a labor contract system with Mexico between the years of 1942 to 1964. Chávez believed in non-violent tactics and advocated for passive resistance. Therefore his tactics included grassroots organizing, strikes, protests, marches, boycotts and hunger strikes. The UFW took the national stage in 1965 when they began a California Grape Boycott that eventually exerted far-reaching economic pressure from the East Coast to even Europe when labor unions joined in support of the UFW. The UFW and the leadership of Chávez and Huerta inspired Chicanos across the country to become active participants in the fight for social justice—they are icons of *Chicanismo*. César Chávez is now acknowledged with an official state holiday in California, Colorado and Texas. His image was placed on a U.S. postal stamp and even Apple computers used his image to sell their products. In 2012, the UFW celebrates their 50th anniversary—they are a testament to not only the legacy of the Chicano Movement, but to the power of social justice in our everyday lives.

The UFW has a long-standing relationship with the Northeast San Fernando Valley because of its agricultural past, but also because the Mexican/Chicano communities historically supported their organizing efforts. In 1994, San Fernando became the first city in the United States to declare a holiday for César Chávez according to resident Everto Ruiz, who also explained that during the Grape Boycott the UFW sent organizer Paul Espinoza to live and organize in San Fernando. And the new local high school (straddling San Fernando, Pacoima and Sylmar) was named in 2011 as the César E. Chávez Learning Academies.

For the past nineteen years, the area has sponsored a César Chávez March and Festival in support of the UFW and the legacy of César Chávez. The march usually begins in Pacoima and ends in Mission Hills

César E. Chavez Memorial.
San Fernando, CA.
Photo: Javier Martinez

Dolores Huerta speaking at the César E. Chávez Annual March, 2009. San Fernando, CA. Photo: Javier Martinez

THE CHICANA/O ART MOVEMENT

The Chicano art movement was tied to the Chicano civil rights movement of the late 1960s and early 1970s. It visualized a Chicano cultural identity based on "resistance and affirmation." The use of "cultural space" within the barrio was one of the tools used to challenge the dominant culture, as empty walls in the community were converted to canvases for artistic expression. The Chicano mural movement was "community based" and the community decided what they wanted on the walls as they reclaimed their cultural heritage through art. Murals were painted all over the barrios of the Southwest and they became both a method of social commentary and education, as well as a celebration of cultural pride. Chicano public art was political and it was able to express a cultural identity often overlooked by the dominant society. Most importantly, the art movement identified certain cultural symbols as sources for Chicano art; it created a visual language for the Chicano movement and *Chicanismo*. These murals transformed dominant perceptions of Chicanos both within and outside those communities. As Sanchez-Tranquilino (1990) explains:

> Chicano murals go beyond signifying artistic accomplishment, they stand as a testament to the capacity of U.S. Mexicans to organize, plan and direct themselves toward the process of social change and the production of art… In particular, the prolific creation of murals represented successful collective efforts on the part of the community toward national self-definition through political and cultural activism. As they put into effect the ideals of Chicano liberation through this organizing process, artists and members of the Mexican American communities served to educate each other, while also educating non-Chicanos (pg. 93).

Furthermore, a new Chicano aesthetics was created during this time period that had at its center the lived environment or everyday reality of Chicanos as the inspiration for the art. Tomas Ybarra-Frausto (1990) labeled the art "*un nuevo arte del pueblo* (a new art of the people) created from shared experience and based on communal art traditions" and as such, "cultural practices of everyday life were seen as nutrient sources for Chicano art forms" (pgs. 57-59). This *nuevo arte del*

at Brand Park. In 2004, San Fernando dedicated the César E. Chávez Memorial Park (designed by local artist Ignacio Garcia), a permanent celebration of the life and work of Chávez, and it also ensures that future generations will learn of his legacy. According to the official press release:

> The Memorial is the largest and most intricate monument in the Nation that honors the great civil rights and labor leader, César E. Chávez. The Memorial consists of a fountain, a bronze sculpture of Chávez, a sculpture of ten farm workers, and a 100 foot mural, placed in a 23,000 square foot park-like setting that together educates and provides an opportunity for reflection on the significance of Chávez's life.

pueblo used artistic folk forms found in our Mexican heritage, such as *pulqueria* art (colorful public murals); *Estampas* (chromo-lithographed calendar); *altares* (altars); *almanaques* (chromo-lithographed calendar); and Chicano artistic folk forms such as graffiti, tattoos, pinto art, and lowrider art (pgs. 59-61). The aesthetics of this new art movement created a visual language that linked the histories and cultures of Chicanos (pre-Columbian, Mexican and American) based on a collective consciousness that engaged revolutionary and political struggle against the dominant culture. It was an example of Chicanos using cultural space to create a cultural identity on their own terms—which expressed an inherent rage filled with passion, resistance and affirmation.

RUSHING WATERS, RISING DREAMS

The legacy of the Chicana/o art movement is apparent in the themes of the artwork in *Rushing Waters, Rising Dreams*. Many of the artists draw their inspiration from the previous one, "el nuevo arte del pueblo," but they also explore themes such as healing, *Indigenismo*, cultural identity, gender, neighborhood, and history. The artists Raul Herrera, Rick Ortega, Erica Friend, and Ramiro Alejandro Hernandez (R@H) explore in their art MesoAmerican culture and spirituality. In the process, they are educating a new generation about the need to re-connect to those teachings and ways of living.

Just like many of the artists during the Chicano Movement, many of the artists work as both individuals and collectives—the year 2011 saw the creation of the 818 Valley Ratz and the San Fernando Cultural Arts Collective (SFCAC). The SFCAC is "dedicated to promoting culture, artistic creativity, family bonding and neighborhood networking through a bimonthly art walk and other events. By highlighting local artists and supporting small businesses, the SFCAC hopes to strengthen community engagement and revitalize the arts in the northeast San Fernando Valley." The art of Sergio Hernandez (who also attended CSUN) captures social and political commentary on the legacy of Bracero history and César Chávez, as well as referencing current issues such as Mitt Romney or "Meskin

Mitt" (a 2012 Republican Presidential candidate whose family has Mormon roots in Mexico) and the Monsanto controversy (the leading producer of genetically engineered seeds). Also many of the murals included in this book visualize how urban space and public art can be used to create community enabling place by celebrating Chicano icons such as the Mexican artist Frida Kahlo, Mexican American singer Linda Ronstadt, actor Danny Trejo, La Virgen de Guadalupe, Ritchie Valens, and Mary Helen Ponce. All of the art continues the tradition of "resistance and affirmation," as well as articulates a barrio aesthetics that explicitly expresses the culture and history of the Northeast San Fernando Valley. As echoed in the essays, art allows for healing and balance to our psyches and is an integral part of building "empowered communities."

The various essays, interviews, poems, photos, and art in *Rushing Waters, Rising Dreams* reveal many themes, such as the search for cultural identity; the desire to belong and create community with others—creating *place* using urban *space*; the healing role of the arts; the power of education; the need for leadership and activism, especially among the youth; social justice; and the importance of women as leaders, artists and activists in these communities. One of the things that all these authors share is a link to Tia Chucha's. As mentioned in many of the essays and poems, when Tia Chucha's opened in the Northeast San Fernando Valley in 2001 it brought many activists, artists and community members together and it transformed lives—by creating community enabling space and place within the barrio. From the beginning, Tia Chucha's also created a space for writers and poets to share their stories through the creation of Open Mic night; various author readings/book signings; writing workshops; and for the past seven years, the annual *Celebrating Words Festival*. In collecting poetry submissions for this book, we relied on the community of poets connected to Tia Chucha's through Open Mic Night and the women's writing group organized by Jenuine, ITWOW (In the Words of Womyn). Jenuine also contributed an essay to the book that traces her journey to Tia Chucha's, which is now "home" for her, and shares her experiences as a writer and poet.

**Stream of Life. 22x46. Oil on canvas, 2009.
Artist: Rick Ortega. San Fernando, CA.**

The essays by Trini Rodriguez, Karina Ceja, Cozkacuauhtli Huitzilzenteotl, and Yaotl Mazahua share their personal stories of growing up in the Northeast San Fernando Valley, revealing not only the struggles of identity shaped by the forces of one's family and community, but also how education becomes a liberating space. All four of these contributors attended California State University, Northridge (CSUN) and took classes in the Department of Chicana and Chicano Studies. Each one of them were able to bridge the knowledge at the university and connect it to their community through activism. Yaotl, in particular, mentions how music saved his life since as a youth he was attracted to gang culture. Yet music and spirituality allowed him a different way of thinking and acting. Cozkacuauhtli was also drawn to gang culture as a youth, but he found healing and balance through learning, practicing, and teaching *Indigenismo*.

The stories shared by Trini and Karina deal with the impact of gender and the ways that sexism both restricted their lives, but also how they were able to challenge those constructions and empower themselves. A theme that runs throughout this book is the power and contributions of *las mujeres*/the women as elders, leaders, teachers, writers, artists, etc. As Felicia Montes (another graduate of Chicana/o Studies at CSUN) notes in her essay on being an "artivist"—art becomes a tool to "educate, empower, and transform"; it is the work of Xicanistas to create a space for women to heal, create and support their community[-ies]. It is significant to mention that the staff of Tia Chucha's is primarily women and as Chicana writer Cherríe Moraga (1993) notes—this is no coincidence.

> The earth is female. It is no accident then that the main grassroots activists defending the earth, along with Native peoples, are women of all races and cultures. Regardless of the so-called 'advances' of Western 'civiliza-

tion,' women remain the chief caretakers, nurturers, and providers for our children and our elders (pg. 172)

Healing is probably one of the most important lessons of all these stories, yet it is a process that directly ties the individual to the collective and reaches back to the lessons of our MesoAmerican ancestors. It is knowledge and ways of living that have been denied to us through colonization, conquest, and assimilation. Yet as I have often heard Luis J. Rodriguez say, this knowledge is part of our "genetic memory code." We just have to re-connect to it—and to our authentic selves. Art provides us with that direction, inspiration and healing.

THE FUTURE: THE YOUTH

"We cannot seek achievement for ourselves and forget about progress and prosperity for our community... Our ambitions must be broad enough to include the aspirations and needs of others, for their sakes and for our own."
—*César Chávez*

AN EXCITING FEATURE of this book is the inclusion of the voices and perspectives of youth and young adults since they will be the next generation of artists, writers, poets, leaders and activists. It was important to include excerpts from the children's books from San Fernando Valley-based writer René Colato Laínez, who in his work explores such themes as immigration, identity, language, cultural traditions, and family. As he writes on his website: "My goal as a writer is to produce good multicultural children's literature; stories where minority children are portrayed in a positive way, where they can see themselves as heroes, and where they can dream and have hopes for the future. I want to write authentic stories of Latin American children living in the United States." The arts, especially books, can be an important tool for children, especially children of color, to teach them a positive sense of self and hopefully see themselves as part of the American cultural fabric.

A multicultural perspective of neighborhood can be seen in the photo essay by Violet Soto, who uses her camera to document everyday life. Her photos capture the beauty and inspiration of urban space, and by picking up a camera Violet hopes to use her art to educate others to how she sees the world. The essay by Angel F. Hernandez, "A Barrio Playground," documents urban skateboard culture at PRod Skate Park in Pacoima where many youth find self-expression and create community. The essay points to the pressures of gang culture in this neighborhood for young men, but also demonstrates that alternatives do exist. Urban Skateboarding is a way of life, it is an artistic expression for these youth, and skate parks are a much needed resource for their cultural survival.

And, finally, the photo essay on "Young Warriors" demonstrates how some youth in the Northeast San Fernando Valley are picking up the torch and continuing the legacy of activism. With the motto, "Every Youth is a Warrior of Their Own Struggles," the program engages youth to develop the necessary skills and knowledge to make their own lives better, as well as their community[-ies]. All of these essays point to the reality that the arts and education are necessary nutrients for the youth, who are the next leaders and activists. In the stories of these youth, I connect to my own personal journey as they too are embracing the philosophies of "Be the Change You Want in the World," "Power to the People," and "The Personal as Political." Most importantly, the youth in these communities are already contributing to the legacy of barriology to create community enabling space and place in the Northeast San Fernando Valley.

My hope is that this book *Rushing Waters, Rising Dreams* will be the beginning of a larger project of documenting the history of the Northeast San Fernando Valley. There are many more voices that wait to be heard, many more lessons of community survival to be learned, and many more examples of art and activism to be realized. Community histories are an important contribution to actualizing those goals—and as this book strongly suggests—¡La Lucha Continua!—The Struggle Continues.

**César Lives. 2002.
Artist: Sergio
Hernandez**

For a more complete examination of the Chicano Movement, I suggest watching *Chicano!: The History of the Mexican American Civil Rights Movement, Episode 1-4,* (Los Angeles: Distributed by National Latino Communications Center, 1996), video-recording.

REFERENCES

Acuña, Rodolfo F. 2000. *Occupied America: A History of Chicanos, 4th Edition.* New York: Longman.

Acuña, Rodolfo F. 1996. *Anything But Mexican: Chicanos in Contemporary Los Angeles.* London: Verso.

Chávez, Ernesto. 2002. *"Mi Raza Primero!" (My People First!): Nationalism, Identity, and Insurgency in the Chicano Movement in Los Angeles, 1966-1978.* Berkeley: University of California Press.

Cruz, Migdalia. 1993. Rushing Waters: A History Fantasy Play. Commissioned by Cornerstone Theater Company: Los Angeles, CA.

Garcia, Ignacio. 1997. *Chicanismo: The Forging of a Militant Ethos Among Mexican Americans.* Tucson, AZ: University of Arizona Press.

Gaspar de Alba, Alicia. 1998. *Chicano Art Inside/Outside The Master's House: Cultural Politics and the CARA Exhibition.* Austin, TX: University of Texas Press.

Marin, Marguerite V. 1991. *Social Protest in an Urban Barrio: A Study of the Chicano Movement, 1966-1974.* Lanham, MD: University Press of America.

Moraga Cherríe, 1993. *The Last Generation.* Boston, MA: South End Press.

Muñoz Jr., Carlos. 1989. *Youth, Identity, Power in the Chicano Movement.* London, New York: Verso.

Ponce, Mary Helen. 1993. *Hoyt Street: An Autobiography.* Albuquerque: University of New Mexico Press.

Rodriguez, Luis J. 1993. *Always Running: La Vida Loca, Gang Days in L.A.* Willimantic, CT : Curbstone Press.

Sanchez Tranquilino, Marcos. 1990. "Chicano Murals and the Discourses of Art and Americanization." In *Signs from the Heart: California Chicano Murals.* Venice, CA: Social and Public Art Resource Center.

Cockcroft, Eva Sperling, and Holly Barnet-Sanchez. 1993. Signs from the Heart: California Chicano Murals. Venice, CA: Social and Public Art Resource Center.

Villa, Raul Homero. 2000. *Barrio Logos: Space and Place in Urban Chicano Literature and Culture.* Austin, TX: University of Texas Press.

Ybarra-Frausto, Tomás. 1990. "Arte Chicano: Images of a Community". In *Signs From the Heart: California Chicano Murals.* Venice, CA: Social and Public Art Resource Center. San Fernando Valley

Statistics: http://www.csun.edu/sfverc/Data/2004ethnic.html

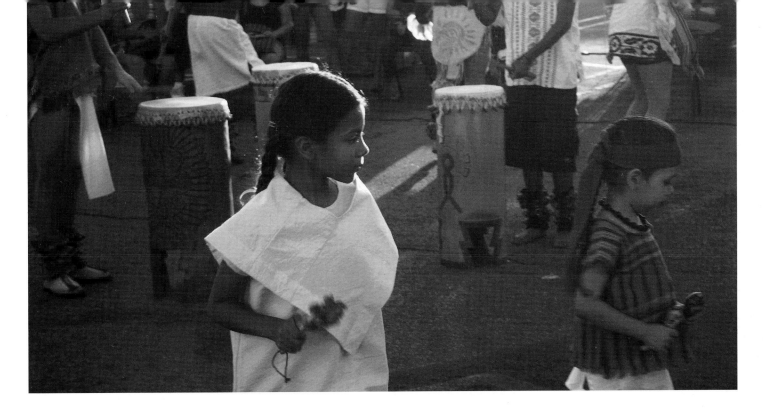

Tia Chucha's Centro Cultural & Bookstore: A Short History

TIA CHUCHA'S WAS FIRST ESTABLISHED in 2001 as a limited liability company with Luis J. Rodriguez and his wife Trini as partners along with their brother-in-law Enrique Sanchez, Chicano artist Otto "Tito" Sturcke, and activist/organizer Maria Flores. With funding from Luis and Trini Rodriguez, and a generous grant from the Liberty Hill Foundation's Social Entrepreneurial Fund, they created a full coffee bar with Mayan motifs, painted in soft earth colors reminiscent of Mexico or Central America, with floors exhibiting amazing tile work (done by a Guatemalan friend) as well as a performance stage area, art gallery, bookshelves, computers, and workshop space in a strip mall in Sylmar, CA.

Known as Tia Chucha's Café Cultural, the place continued (Sturcke and Flores had moved on by then) for about five years in that spot, offering authentic Mexika (so-called Aztec) dance, theater classes (with at least two original theater companies, Mateo Hernandez's E.A.R.T.H. Company and Joe Cedillo's Tres Chingazos), writing workshops, arts training (mostly with their first resident artist, Juan Pueblo), indigenous cosmology, healing arts, community dialogues, art exhibits, film nights, and a weekly free Open Mic

ABOVE:
Danzantes from Temachtia Quetzacoatl. Tia Chucha's, June 2011. Sylmar, CA. Photo: Luz Rodriguez

The existence of Tia Chucha's in the Valley has affirmed the understanding that with a commitment to each other's dignity, we can draw out the talent, beauty and gifts inherent in every person...

(including a monthly Open Mic for Spanish-language poets, singers, and musicians).

Authors that graced the stage include Ruben Martinez, Sandra Cisneros, Victor Villasenor, Adrienne Rich, Lalo Alcaraz, Culture Clash, Wanda Coleman, Father Greg Boyle, Tom Hayden, Michael Meade, Reyna Grande, and others. Bands played here from the larger East L.A. musical scene as well as the Valley, such as Quetzal, Very Be Careful, Domingo Siete, Quinto Sol, Ollin, Aztlan Underground, and La Santa Cecilia—and performers like Charles Wright and the Watts 103rd Street Rhythm Band (famous for the 1960s classic, "Express Yourself"). New groups emerged, such as the Xicano conscious Hip Hop group, El Vuh; traditional Peruvian/Mexican music group Raices; Hijos de la Tierra; folk singers like Big Joe Hurt; and the Spanish language rock group, Noxdie, led by one of our guitar teachers, Alejandro La Borde.

Son Jaracho Group.
El Nido Champions
Gala 2011.
Photo: Luz Rodriguez

Tia Chucha's offered classes in Son Jarocho musical tradition from Veracruz, Mexico (one of our first teachers was Cesar Castro, formerly of Son Madera); Bomba dance from Puerto Rico; hand-made puppetry; indigenous cosmology (Mexikayotl); film nights; healing & healthy living; and eventually establishing their own resident Mexika Danza group called Temachtia Quetzacoatl, run by one of the few women heads, Monique Orozco.

BY 2003, LUIS J. RODRIGUEZ, singer and musicologist Angelica Loa Perez, and Victor Mendoza of Xicano Records & Films, began the nonprofit Tia Chucha's Centro Cultural next door to the cultural café (they received their 501 (c) (3) tax exempt status a year later). Trini now also managed the café/bookstore/gallery/performance space while the nonprofit hired local Sylmar resident Mike Centeno to run the programming. Artists that exhibited work for sale included Gilbert "Magu" Lujan, Chaz Bojorquez, Rick Ortega, Maria Reyna, Sergio Hernandez, Lalo Garcia, and many more—the well-known as well as those starting out.

However, by the end of 2006 the owners of the strip mall almost tripled the rent to make way for a high-tech Laundromat. This forced Tia Chucha's to move to a smaller space in Lake View Terrace, albeit without the coffee bar. They also ended up losing café equipment, refrigerators, deli cases, an ice-making machine, bookshelves, and more when the private warehouse they used to store these got broken into, trashed and robbed.

But Luis and Trini persisted, with the loving help of a growing and active community. In 2009 they found a better space in another strip mall in Sylmar, and in the process revitalized another depressed area.

In 2007, the café's LLC disbanded, donating the books, shelves, computers, files, and more to the nonprofit. Trini became operations director. Luis served as board president, setting up a community board made up of people from white, Asian, Chicano, Central American, and African American communities with ties to funds, resources, and other institutions. Till this day neither Trini nor Luis get paid—Tia Chucha's is their gift to community.

Ruben Guevara, famed Chicano singer/musician

Las Krudas Cubensi, Cuban Hip Hop Group, May 2011. Tia Chucha's. Sylmar, CA.
Photo: Luz Rodriguez

(known for years as performance artist Funkahuatl) became Development Director. Over the years, a staff of mostly young Chicanas and Chicanos helped Trini keep the place organized and happening (among them were Joaquin Chavez, Luz Sanchez, Esperanza Sanchez, Nani Sanchez, Carmen Alarcon, Alicia Barajas, Luz Rodriguez, Arlene Mejorado, Silverio Pelayo, Ray Garcia, Christine Vega, Blanca Boche, Frank Escamilla, Karina Ceja, Stacy Valdez, Margarita Lopez, Melissa Sanvicente, Wendy Pizano, Vanessa Lazaro, Yuri Magana, and more).

Osbaldo Velasquez, Mary Archibald, Gina Perez, and Jorge Gomez have helped with accounting. And key volunteers gave time, technical assistance, and much love, including the go-to-guy Walter P. Little, computer whiz Johnnie Phung, Open Mic emcees Neri Boche and Alfredo Hidalgo, among so many others.

LUIS WAS ALSO ABLE to bring Tia Chucha Press to the Northeast Valley in 2005—and in 2002 to start a CD production project, Dos Manos Records. Beginning in 2006 Tia Chucha's Centro Cultural put on the only annual outdoor literacy & performance festival in the San Fernando Valley with the help of L.A. City's Department of Cultural Affairs. Called "Celebrating Words: Written, Performed or Sung," they featured local artisans, vendors, and community service booths; free book giveaways and book sales; a stage with music, poetry, spoken word, theater, and dance; and panels with authors on writing and similar topics. These festivals have been held at Sylmar Park, Carrizo Park, and Los Angeles Mission College. In addition, Tia Chucha's incorporated a youth empowerment project called Young Warriors, often working with probation and other troubled youth, begun by a 17-year-old young Pacoima resident named Mayra Zaragoza and 19-year-old Sylmar resident Brian Dessaint.

National media attention to Luis's writing and work with Tia Chucha's appeared in NBC's "Nightly News with Brian Williams"; CNN's "What Matters;" Head Line News' "Leaders with Heart;" PBS-TV's Jim Lehrer News Hour; BBC Radio; *People Magazine (en Espanol)*; *the Huffington Post*; *Los Angeles Times*; *L.A. Daily News*; *La Opinion*, *Christian Science Monitor*, and many local and national radio outlets.

Other recognition included "Local Heroes of the Community" awards from KCET-TV and Union Bank of California to Trini, Enrique, and Luis. *La Opinion* Spanish-language newspaper also designated Trini as a "Mujer Destacada" (Outstanding Woman). And Luis was honored with "An Unsung Hero of Compassion" award by the Wisdom in Action Foundation, presented by his Holiness, the Dalai Lama; "A Season for Nonviolence Hero" award from the Agape Spiritual Center; and a "Ruben Salazar/Spirit of Struggle" award from Inner City Struggle of East Los Angeles.

By 2012, Tia Chucha's Centro Cultural & Bookstore had more than a quarter-of-a-million-dollar budget with invitations to do satellites in Boyle Heights/East L.A. and possibly Chicago. It is now known across the United States and in countries like Japan, England, Germany, other parts of Europe, as well as El Salvador, Guatemala, Venezuela, Peru, Argentina, and Mexico (where Tia Chucha's was replicated during Mexico City's 2006 Book Fair and where they established the first Lowrider Car & Bike show at the 2009 Guadalajara International Book Festival).

As its namesake, like Tia Chucha's there is no other.

> **...At the same time, the continued struggle to sustain Tia Chucha's has shown me that communities should not have to compete for resources and support for something as basic as a quality of life that includes identifying and expanding the very gifts everyone is born with.**
>
> –Trini Rodriguez

Tia Chucha
A 1991 poem
by Luis Rodriguez

Every few years Tia Chucha
would visit the family
in a tornado of song and open us up
as if we were an overripe avocado.
She was a dumpy, black-haired
creature of upheaval who often
    came unannounced
with a bag of presents, including homemade
    perfumes and colognes that smelled
    something like
rotting fish on a hot day at the tuna cannery.

They said she was crazy. Oh sure, she once
    ran out naked
to catch the postman with a letter that didn't
    belong to us.
I mean, she had this annoying habit
    of boarding city buses
and singing at the top of her voice—one bus driver
even refused to go on until she got off.

But crazy?

To me, she was the wisp of the wind's freedom,

a music-maker who once tried to teach me guitar
but ended up singing and singing,
me listening, and her singing
until I put the instrument down
and watched the clock click the lesson time away.

I didn't learn guitar, but I learned something
about her craving for the new, the unbroken,
so she could break it. Periodically
    she banished herself
from the family—and was the better for it.

I secretly admired Tia Chucha.
She was always quick with a story,
another "Pepito" joke or a hand-written lyric
that she would produce regardless of the occasion.

She was a despot of desire,
uncontainable as a splash of water
on a varnished table.

I wanted to remove the layers
of unnatural seeing,
the way Tia Chucha beheld
the world, with first eyes,
like an infant who can discern
the elixir within milk.

I wanted to be one of the prizes
she stuffed into her rumpled bag.

The Healing Power
of the Arts

By Trini Rodriguez

Creativity is healing. I can attest to that personally. At Tia Chucha's, I've had the opportunity to write from the heart along with other women. I'm inspired daily by amazing women in a fearless search of their better selves, seeking answers and collaborating with others to that end.

I AM GRATEFUL to have helped create the unique cultural arts and literacy space known as Tia Chucha's. Conceived over ten years ago as a cafe/bookstore, it's now a non-profit cultural center/bookstore and community-driven hub-oasis of creative arts, expression, and empowerment in the Northeast San Fernando Valley. Tia Chucha's tagline, "Where Art & Minds Meet – For a Change," once just an idea, is now a lived experience for those who have learned to tap into their reservoir of creative energy at the Centro. The struggle to create a space where art transforms community is both an individual and collective challenge. As it would happen, Tia Chucha's has been central to my own process of transformation, compelling me to step beyond my own assumed limits. My experience mirrors that of those who have allowed themselves to heal, change, and grow in the process of imagining fuller lives for themselves and their communities.

When Tia Chucha's first opened its doors, the last thing I wanted was to become the operations director of such a promising and necessary place. The responsibility felt too demanding. My shoulders were heavy with

emotional baggage. I was haunted by a past of injured confidence and stifled dreams. My experience growing up in the Valley fed a notion that I shouldn't expect much in my life, and consequently I behaved in diminished ways.

I grew up in working class Pacoima. My neighborhood was full of people who were expected to stay in their place and not rock any boats. We had our roles, and those roles were not to be questioned. By the time I graduated from San Fernando High School I was familiar with doing what I was told. Strict traditional parents—who managed to provide for and keep all of their eleven kids in line—had raised me. And my mom and dad, informed by their own experience and guided by love or fear or both, insisted that my future was only to get married and have kids. Just live. Work hard. Then die. Be practical. Don't dream big. Even my spirit knew there had to be more, but what?

In school I earned straight A's. Buckling down to study was more a pattern than a path; it was what I did to prove I had value, while feeling purposeless. Even though my father and uncle helped construct what is now Cal State University at Northridge (CSUN), neither of them felt entitled to encourage us, their own family, to pursue a higher education in the very buildings they helped create. They too were products of their experiences and time. We could build, we could care for, we could be the solid foundation of this place called the Valley… we were supposed to contribute, yet not expect much in return, not question our roles, not escape our station.

But things were about to change.

IT WAS 1971. I was a young first-generation female citizen of Mexican descent, set to graduate in June. The world around me was rocking with change. A local college recruiter, a friend of the family, paid a visit to my parents to ask them to let me go to college. Stanford University wanted me. Other colleges did too. My older brother had gone to UCLA. But I was a daughter with no experience thinking for or standing up for myself. Instead, my oldest sister advocated for me. But it was no use—my parents' answer was like stone: No.

The battle was not over. The Chicano Movement was in full swing. The fight for education and our place in society was on. All of us, males and females, were urged to flex our imaginations, to go farther to improve ourselves and come back to improve our communities. The recruiters, my counselors and others persisted. Finally my parents conceded to let me attend CSUN on one condition: I would live at home. However, by my last year of college I felt suffocated. I wanted to move out and live on my own. Still I wanted my parents' blessing; I kept asking for permission. Again: No. Then, surprising even myself, at 21 years of age I dared to assume authority over my life. I left home without permission— and for that I was summarily disowned. Thankfully, I still had the emotional support of my many siblings and relatives. Thus, I began a harsh yet crucial journey of self and social discovery. It was a path I walked for close to twenty years without my parents.

A year after leaving home, I graduated *cum laude*, the first female in my family to earn a college degree. Seeking and growing, questioning and learning, is like satisfying a hunger. Education sparked my curiosity. Everywhere I found people equally inspired by change and social justice. I became a bilingual teacher, actively involved in the quest for quality education, integration and equal representation. To be seen, appreciated and heard. I wanted these things for myself; I wanted these things for everyone.

Even with my active life, I was constantly reminded that I was a disowned, unwelcomed daughter. The rejection proved debilitating. I felt worthless. So in 1983 I jumped at the invitation to be on the editorial board of a national newspaper advocating for the rights of undocumented workers. I moved to Chicago, where I continued my social activism. It was there that I reconnected with and eventually married my husband Luis, and where I gave birth to my two sons, Ruben and Chito. By June of 2000, we moved back to California, returning to family. As it turned out, we lived in the Pacoima house I grew up in. I had come full circle. I had come home.

But the difference between the Valley and Chicago was staggering. In Chicago, we were surrounded by neighborhoods filled with music, poetry, and cultural arts. In contrast, the Valley seemed to be in a state of paralysis, numbed into complacency, as if nothing had changed. We were disappointed, but not disheartened. My husband Luis, my brother-in-law Enrique, and myself had been part of the groundswell of changes that had come about in the 1970s and beyond. Soon we decided to do something about this neglect in the Valley. Our families and kids deserved better. Something had to be done to awaken the possibility of a change. The arts and literacy, with their blend of creativity and consciousness, could be the catalysts for enhancing the quality of life for our beleaguered communities. We just had to be willing to draw out the beauty that lay dormant under the seemingly barren Valley. With this commitment, the dream and struggle for Tia Chucha's began.

CREATING A VITAL COMMUNITY SPACE was no small feat. Finding a suitable location was fraught with headaches, and acquiring permits an endless obstacle course. After six months of paying rent we finally opened the doors to Tia Chucha's in December of 2001. When in March we had a grand opening event, the community came out in droves. They were excited. Curious. Joyous. At last—a space to celebrate the community, its art, its people, its own way. A place to talk. Meet. Discuss new ideas. Go beyond the expected.

Since that time, thousands of people have gathered,

The arts and literacy, with their blend of creativity and consciousness, could be the catalysts for enhancing the quality of life for our beleaguered communities. We just had to be willing to draw out the beauty that lay dormant under the seemingly barren Valley.

connected, learned, grown within the embrace of Tia Chucha's intentional environment. In spite of having changed location three times in the area of Sylmar, the welcoming nature of the center has remained intact. Everyone is invited to participate and learn. People become aware that life can be more than just going to work, staying at home, or just being spectators. They come to know they can be active participants in the shaping of their own lives, in impacting their communities for the better. Here all are invited to step out of the shadows and be seen—where a microphone is for sharing your voice as well as listening to someone else's. Here one can express and connect with people who are

Copalera.
Photography &
Graphic Design,
2009. Artist:
Raul Herrera.
San Fernando, CA.

making a difference. Here art, workshops, talks, film screenings, theatre, books and creativity are stepping stones to discover more of yourself and what you have to offer the world. It is a place to heal and become more of what you were born to be.

I have seen many people change and grow because of Tia Chucha's—from staff and volunteers, to family and friends, to customers and new acquaintances. I have seen young women break out of their shells in song, dance, poetry—finding the courage to speak up, and feel complete. I have seen young men open their hearts, humbled to their truths, and left feeling better about themselves than before. I have seen adult men, old men, grown women and older women find their wisdom and gifts in ways they have waited a life-time to discover. And I've seen children witness a space filled with creativity, unaware that this is not the way it has always been, even though it should be.

Many times I've heard people say, "I wish there had been a place like this when I was growing up." If I had been exposed to a center like Tia Chucha growing up, perhaps I would have felt whole sooner, been more aware sooner, dreamt bigger sooner.

Tia Chucha's has given me a new set of experiences that allow me to appreciate the Valley and myself more than ever. Like others, I too have changed as a result of Tia Chucha's—partly by necessity, partly by choice. As full-time volunteer operations director, I'm required to go beyond my limited view of myself. I now realize—sometimes after I have already done what I thought I couldn't—that together with others we are capable of reinventing a fuller version of our world and ourselves. Creativity is healing. I can attest to that personally. At Tia Chucha's, I've had the opportunity to write from the heart along with other women. I'm inspired daily by amazing women in a fearless search of their better selves, seeking answers and collaborating with others to that end.

About fifteen years ago, a Dine (Navajo) medicine man Anthony Lee, and his wife Delores, spiritually adopted me on the largest Native American reservation in the United States. Luis brought me to these tradi-tions, which helped him connect to his own Tarahu-mara native roots and in becoming clean and sober after twenty-seven years of drugs and alcohol. These traditions also touched back to my own roots among the Huichol tribe in Jalisco, Mexico.

SANCTIONED BY ANTHONY LEE as well as elders among the Lakota, Mexika, and other peoples, Luis and I—with family members and friends—started two sweat lodge circles around ten years ago in Pacoima and in San Fernando. One still remains and I presently pour water at a monthly women's sweat lodge ceremony, where healing takes the form of coming together in in-digenous song, prayer, and humility to face our deepest wounds and come out stronger and wiser as a result. Though not officially part of Tia Chucha's, this sweat lodge is only five minutes away and anyone who's in-terested is invited to take part, which many Tia Chucha staff, instructors, volunteers, and participants have done over the years.

My time at Tia Chucha's has shown me that having creative, healing, and welcoming artistic/literary spaces are critical to our need as humans to find new ways of being and becoming. I am the last person who would have suspected that art transforms community. Now I know that it does. The arts are not a luxury. They are a necessity. For all of us are artists of one form or another.

RIGHT:
Cosmic Journey.
Graphic Design (Digital Mural-Codex), 2010.
Artist: Raul Herrera

BELOW:
Orgullo Mexicano/
Mexican Pride. 1979
Chevrolet Monte
Carlo. C & L Customs.
UCE Car Club.
Veteran's Park,
Sylmar, CA.
Photo: Estevan Oriol

Chicana/o Art
in the
Northeast
San Fernando
Valley

ABOVE LEFT:
Xochiquetzal. 42x58
Oil on canvas, 2009.
Artist: Rick Ortega.
San Fernando, CA.

ABOVE RIGHT:
Las Muertas De Juarez.
18x24 Oil on canvas,
2011. Artist: Erica Friend.
Sylmar, CA.

RIGHT:
Omeyocan. 44x58
Oil on wood, 2010.
Artist: Rick Ortega.
San Fernando, CA.

LEFT: Chantico. 45x56
Oil on canvas, 2010.
Artist: Rick Ortega.
San Fernando, CA.

BELOW: Xochipilli. 15x30
Oil on canvas, 2011.
Artist: Erica Friend.
Sylmar, CA.

RIGHT:
Mural. Alley on Glenoaks and Paxton. Pacoima, CA. Photo: Javier Martinez.

BELOW LEFT:
Finding A Balance. 16x20 Acrylic on canvas, 2012. Artist: Ramiro Alejandro Hernandez (R@H). San Fernando Valley artist.

BELOW RIGHT:
Blue Goddess. 16x20 Acrylic on canvas, 2011. Artist: Ramiro Alejandro Hernandez (R@H). San Fernando Valley artist.

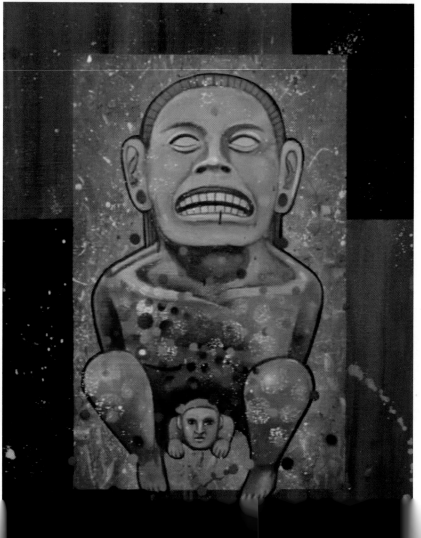

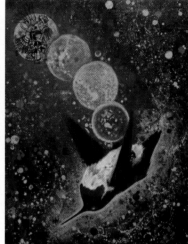

LEFT:
Goddess of Death. 18x22
Acrylic and Aerosol on canvas,
2011. Artist: Ramiro Alejandro
Hernandez (R@H). San
Fernando Valley artist.

ABOVE:
Huitzilopochtli Death. 11x14
Oil and Aerosol on canvas,
2011. Artist: Erica Friend.
Sylmar, CA.

ABOVE LEFT:
Mural. Linda Ronstadt, Canciones
de Mi Padre. Pacoima, CA.
Photo: Javier Martinez

ABOVE RIGHT:
Mural on Van Nuys Boulevard.
Pacoima, CA.
Photo: Javier Martinez

RIGHT:
Mural on Van Nuys Boulevard.
Pacoima, CA.
Photo: Javier Martinez

ABOVE:
Mural. Chacon's Barber Shop.
Artists: Juan Pueblo and Donna
Reyes. San Fernando, CA.
Photo: Javier Martinez.

LEFT:
Mural. Williams Furniture Shop
(details: Ritchie Valens and
Mary Helen Ponce).
Pacoima,CA.
Photo: Javier Martinez

ABOVE LEFT:
César E. Chávez
Memorial.
Artist: Ignacio Gomez.
San Fernando, CA.
Photo: Javier Martinez

ABOVE RIGHT:
Bracero Repatriation.
1975.
Artist: Sergio Hernandez

RIGHT:
César E. Chávez Mural
(detail).
Artist: Ignacio Gomez.
San Fernando, CA.
Photo: Javier Martinez

Through My Lens
La Vida

A photo essay
by Violet Soto

AS TOLD TO
DENISE M. SANDOVAL

A lot of my pictures are of nature and industrialization. I like both. I like living in an urban area surrounded by people, but at the same time I like nature a lot.

MY NAME IS VIOLET SOTO and I am 17 years old. I grew up in the Northeast San Fernando Valley. I am a photographer and I take a lot of photos capturing the Latino culture out here and in Los Angeles. I started taking pictures at age 13. I really wanted a camera and my mom bought me a camera that one of her friends was selling for like fifteen dollars. So I started taking pictures of my pets, animals or my family. I never envisioned being a photographer. But I remember when I went to Disneyland with my sister and niece, and my sister wanted me to take a picture of them. Back in the day, she was into photography, but she didn't have the eye for it. *Entonces*, she explained to me about composition. She told me that I was getting too much of the trees and not enough of my sister and niece. And that got me thinking—it changed my point of view of how I took pictures. I saw everything differently. I was fascinated with composition and taking pictures. I took so many pictures constantly. I would be at Tia Chucha's and I would take pictures of everything.

Violet Soto. Photo: Estevan Oriol

When I first started taking pictures, I always shot black and white. I didn't like color—I liked black and white. The contrasts look more dramatic in black and white. It gets you thinking more about the photo when it's in black and white.

CLOCKWISE FROM
TOP LEFT, FACING PAGE:
1- Intersection of Van Nuys
Boulevard and Arleta. Pacoima,
CA. 2- My Neighbor's Backyard.
Symlar, CA. 3- Danzante/Tattoo
Artist. Humphrey Park. Pacoima,
CA. 4- Waitresses at El Jacalito
Restaurant. Pacoima, CA.
5-An Alley in Sylmar.

35

RIGHT:
Mujer de
Mallinahli/Woman
of the Herbs-Plants.
Pacoima, CA.

BOTTOM LEFT:
El Violinista de Van
Nuys Boulevard.
Pacoima, CA.

BOTTOM RIGHT:
La Psycho-Billy
Mujer. Sylmar, CA.

IN THE END, taking pictures makes me feel better about life. Seeing the world through different angles and compositions…it's a whole different kind of world. Sometimes people live here, but they don't see it. So I like to document life, so people can see my point of view.

LEFT: My Backyard. Sylmar, CA.

BELOW: Underneath San Fernando Road. Pacoima, CA.

Movement, Milpas y Mujeres

L.A Artivists who Educate, Empower & Transform

BY FELICIA "FE" MONTES

EDUCATE, AGITATE, ORGANIZE—the rallying cry for 1960s counter culture and the civil rights movement has changed some in 2012… that is for some Southern California based Chican@ and Xican@ artists. From East Los to the San Fernando Valley a vision that is manifested in not much more than a phrase is, "Educate, Empower, Transform"—and this is used by an army of Artivists, Adelitas, Mujeres de Maiz, and ZapARtistas from across Aztlan. As Generation X or "Generation Mex," as artist Lalo Alcaraz names us in one of his cartoons "La Cucaracha," we are the daughters and sons of the Chican@ movement and the generation that has benefitted from its work. As *artivists* we are both artists and activists and our creations are mainly "activist based" with an intent to educate, empower and transform. We have also been fighting on various fronts the devastating battle to keep things in balance for our gente. There have been too many losses of much of what was gained from the civil rights movement of the 1960s and 1970s and our people often struggle to maintain a dignified life.

Education is key to our communities. Many of us are often pushed out of educational institutions, do not finish high school, much less attend college or beyond. If we are lucky we are able to connect to our culture, have a strong base at home, and find key people or places in our lives that support us and give us that extra push of self-esteem, self love and also culture and politics. They empower us to be who we want to be, who our ancestors prayed and dreamt us to be. Mujeres de Maiz (MDM) and Tia Chucha's Centro Cultural (or TC's) hold these visions and teachings close. Both are spaces or better put, states of mind, heart and spirit that manifest education, empowerment and transformation. Walking in to TC's or a MDM event one is forever transformed, one can learn more about yourself, grow and hopefully become a better person. A person who understands self, family and community and works for the betterment of all. A person and gente who educate, empower and transform.

This is what I/we do as Xicana Indigena cultural

In Lak Ech.
Photo:
Azul DelGrasso

activists—educate, empower and transform myself and others and it's a lifelong process, not something learned in one workshop, or one class, etc. I have spent years attempting to combine my academic, artistic, and political life and create, perform, and share my and our creations with others. Through my calling as an artist-educator-organizer, I/we use art and knowledge to educate, inform, and call others to action regarding various social justice issues including education and women's and indigenous rights. My academic and artistic endeavors, including two Master's degrees and the co-creation of two art collectives, have allowed me to push beyond borders and guidelines to weave together varied visions including organizing and programming with art and communities. This work has mainly focused on women's groups specifically two groundbreaking women's art collectives in Los Angeles, *In Lak Ech* and *Mujeres de Maiz*, or women of the corn. In Lak Ech is a Mayan concept meaning "you are my other me" or in Spanish, "*tu eres mi otro yo.*" We understand it to mean that we are all related and that we are all reflections of each other. This is a key concept and mindset in community work such as that of MDM and TC.

Both collectives educate, empower and transform and use art, activism and spirituality as their main forms of education, empowerment and transformation. In Lak Ech, in the flesh, is a performance poetry and song collective of Xicana multi-media artists, writers, educators, and organizers who tell Her-story through poetry, song and drum. In Lak Ech is comprised of Marisol Torres, Felicia Montes, Claudia Mercado, Cristina Gorocica, Rachel Thorson Véliz, Liza Hita, and Marlene Beltran. Their flowering words, which express their urban Xicana Indigena realities are offered to the past, present, and future generations. Since their birth on International Women's Day 1997, they have been heard from the jungles of Chiapas to the concrete jungles of Mexico City, Los Angeles, and beyond. In Lak Ech has traveled throughout California and the southwest to give voice to the many who struggle for dignity, culture, and life. Through canto, comedy, poetry, and observation, they are a unique blend of modern day oral tradition, exploring politics, spirituality, love, and pain. Based in Los Angeles, California, the women of In Lak Ech not only perform poetry and song, but also organize cultural celebrations, participate in conferences, and conduct workshops for diverse communities. These performances have been used as tools for expression, healing, communication, and organizing at various community centers, festivals, high schools, universities, and indigenous ceremonies. In Lak Ech utilizes words to bring awareness and empowerment to the issues of women, family, humanity, and mother earth. As a result, In Lak Ech is the seed that has inspired creative women circles such as Mujeres de Maiz. Both collectives have become a significant presence particularly in Southern California and East Los Angeles through art shows, performances, and organizing efforts including zine publications, all woman events, and representing across the southern California Chican@ cultural circles including at Tia Chucha's. In 2000, In Lak Ech was part

As *artivists,* we are both artists and activists and our creations are mainly "activist based" with an intent to educate, empower and transform.

of a benefit CD for the Peace and Dignity Journeys on the Xican@ Records and Film (XRF) label based in Sylmar. In August 2007, In Lak Ech shared its first spoken word and music CD also put out on XRF.

Mujeres de Maiz is a collective of, by and for the people, specifically urban women of color. The group started among the writings of empowering mentors, where the penetrating power of Xicanisma and important historical lessons and stories were shared through women's creations and thereby planted in the hearts, minds, and spirits of las Mujeres de Maiz. The books housed at Tia Chucha's are those same books that made lasting impact in las Mujeres de Maiz. These include books like: *The Last Generation* by Cherrie Moraga, *Massacre of the Dreamers* by Ana Castillo, and *Borderlands* by Gloria Anzaluda. The influence, inspiration, and empowerment of this women's art and literature has had a profound impact on various generations and together Mujeres de Maiz has created a much needed space for an intercultural, intergenerational, interdisciplinary style, energy, and vida.

In 1997 Mujeres de Maiz, a women of color creative art collective based on activism and personal, artistic, and spiritual growth, was born. Since its beginnings, Mujeres de Maiz has become a groundbreaking force within Los Angeles Chican@, artist, and activist cir-

In Lak Ech is a Mayan concept meaning "you are my other me" or in Spanish, "tu eres mi otro yo." We understand it to mean that we are all related and that we are all reflections of each other.

cles. Mujeres de Maiz (MDM) evolved as an open collective of creative women of color with no membership, no fee, and no initiation. It is an outlet, a space and venue for creative endeavors. It is also a women's circle, an organizing collective, an activist group, and a network of creative women for support as artists of various mediums. In the MDM zine from 1996, Mujeres de Maiz prides themselves on being many things, including a "source of empowerment..." and a "safe space for all women to share their expression and gain support in their projects and lives."

The group has pushed past many borders to create sacred space for women to share their thoughts, experiences, prayers, and politics through the arts and to push theory into flesh. Mujeres de Maiz is where emerging and established women of colors artists share the same stage and page. A group where intergenerational, intercultural and interdisciplinary work is applauded and encouraged, and where a myriad of women of color from different cultures, generations, spiritualities and traditions, come together to honor themselves and all women. It is a place that for many years was the only one of its kind, having been the home and start of many of Los Angeles' women performing Artivists, and where many have shared their creations for the first time and later come to publish and tour their work. In honor of International Women's Day (March 8th), Mujeres de Maiz creates an annual live art show and publication in solidarity with thousands of women across the world, who march for women's rights and important issues. In Los Angeles, the women of this open collective march, pray, organize, and share their gifts, their sacred worlds, words, music, and art... themselves. In these turbulent and changing times, Mujeres de Maiz continues to create, in the words of the Zapatistas, "a world where many worlds fit." As an audience member, Xochitl Palomera stated, "This wombmyn encompasses the true essence of public education. It's the pedagogy used in pre-Hispanic indigenous way of life. You are the Professoras of then and Now... Your work has made a difference in my life." Skrybe, one of the original performers at Mujeres de Maiz, states MDM's intent in another way: "Even if it's just that one" meaning that we share in hopes that it connects, educates, empowers and/or transforms just one person... and more often than not it does to hundreds more including ourselves.

In Lak Ech and Mujeres de Maiz—and the many individuals and other collectives associated with both across Los Angeles—have attended, supported, or performed at various Tia Chucha's events at all three San Fernando Valley locations. Mujeres de Maiz poets and In Lak Ech members have been involved in sharing at the Friday night open-mics, have featured at the annual Celebrating Words festivals, as well as been a part of the first circles of Aztec Dance and son jarocho classes. We continue to work in solidarity with the extended Tia Chucha's (TC) family because TC's is so connected to our own vision of creating a holistically healthy community that is based in arts, activism, culture, and spirit. These tenets are key to both Tia Chucha's and Mujeres de Maiz and weave our work together like a sacred bundle that we hold close. Our programming is our medicine, our poems and instruments, our tools for healing, our books and zines—our codices. As the Hopi elders say, "We are the ones we've been waiting for"—and the time for educating, empowering and transforming is NOW!

Mujeres de Maiz Zine.
Courtesy of
Felicia "Fe" Montes.

Without a
Vision

BY JENNIFER "JENUINE" ALUMBAUGH

*(March 2011—on the occasion of
Tia Chucha's 10th Anniversary)*

without a vision, the people perish

community
is the unity
of art and minds
meeting for a change

community
is the unity
of needs and hope
becoming a vision

community
is the unity
of compassion
and justice
joining in revolution

a change
of perspective
a vision
of healing
a revolution
of the soul

without a vision, the people perish

Mother's
Garden

BY MICHAEL RAY J

I picked these flowers with you in mind,
Wrapped them up in silver twine,
Plucked them from their golden chord
And thus they wither more and more.

Within each petal I saw a thought,
A holy message written and wrought;
Cast down from angels both bought and sold
Then packaged by 12 year olds.

I picked these flower with you in mind
For they reflect the beauty of thine eyes.
Wide and open as Arizona morning skies
And blue as Bisbee azurite mines.

I picked these flower with you in mind
I picked them not knowing that you would mind.

Truth, the real shortcut

BY MIKE DE LA ROCHA

There are moments when I want to give up,
Moments when I don't want to organize anymore,
Moments when I wonder, "Is it really worth it?"
I mean really –
Is it really worth it?

And every time these thoughts slowly creep
    into my mind,
I remember my mother who struggled in
    the delivery room
Hoping that miracles didn't just happen in the Bible.

I remember my Nana Daria who had to work no less
    than 14 hours in the
Hot fields of California to simply provide food
    and shelter for
My aunts and uncles,

I remember my abuelo who came over as a bracero
    in the 1940's,
A farm laborer forced to work for pennies, helping
    corporations become
Wealthy on the backs of his own family,

I remember my Nana Cuca who was a seamstress
    silently sewing dreams of
My family together in a dimly lighted sweatshop in
    downtown Los Angeles,

And then finally, I think of my baby daughter –
I think of what kind of world will I leave her?
What kind of values and morals will I help instill in her?
What kind of person will she say her Daddy was?

And when I think of all that,
I realize that I have no other choice,
I have no other option –

You see, truth is the real shortcut,
Truth does not hide behind walls or borders,
Truth does not manipulate or lie,

Truth is that smile you get from your partner when
there seems like there's no other way,
Truth is knowing that god is talking to you when your
dreams and actions become one,
Truth is that gut instinct that you feel when you are on
the right side of righteousness.

Ya I have my moments when I want to give up,
And then I remember my family,
I remember my community,
I remember my unwavering belief that
Truth is in fact the real shortcut.

Concrete
Incarceration

By Leonel Estrada Chaidez

Do people change
During incarceration
Do they take advantage of the opportunity
To re-think their inner self through POETRY
Putting their thoughts and emotions on a sheet of paper
Instead of creating anger and frustration
Which becomes apparent when looking in the mirror
Poetry has become my way of dealing with my
    incarceration
To work through the hardships of life and love......

The days and nights of isolation
When you're unable to escape
The thought of dying
Death would be my only embrace

I've become broken with sorrow
I've become lost without a proper place
The sounds of chains
The concrete walls
The soul remains
Love there is none...

Poetry came to me
When I needed to express myself the most
In a way where people would listen and understand
My way of life

Scarred
Sisters

By Felicia "Fe" Montes

Like my scarred sisters, Luis Rodri, and those
    of the pelon nation
I am "Always Running"
But I'm still waiting to exhale
Repirar profundamente
Y admirar el sol en mi luna

Crazy curls cover my under construction self
The sign reads, "Women at Work"
To remodel this cold casa
Una mujer de todos
Y de nadie

Conocida por todos
Pero nadie la conoce

Como Frida, mujer, artista, revolucionaria.

Pero hay mucho mas adentro de esta mujer de maiz
De un movimiento madre y papa preacher
Of red rhetoric which she tries to live

Within her sangre of una linea de mujeres ardientes,
    valientes
Con amor, paz y dignidad

Como the homegirl on the corner
Not esperando un vato, un ride
No, she slices vida en quarters
Places them in plastic
And adds her own special juices

She is sweet sixteen, never time nor feria
    for una quinceniera
She stands Sunkist hair tied back in her fashion

veinte uno gear
Sonrisa-white platforms to match

Standing in no-man's land, she cuts her day in half
Escuela y trabajo
Attempting to cortar the ties of her Tia macho
And peel off the watching eyes of mother
And Man-handling stares of men who pass by
Throwing ojos and signs of a language she is just
    beginning to understand

As her homegirls pass her by, on the way to
    some party…
The one she always misses

Cuz she at the corner, Cortando cucumbers
En la esquina esperando clientes,
At the fruit stand, letting them all pass her by.

Like that little woman, mujercita of nine or ten
Who today led a marcha
With pigtails, smile, and eyes of hope
All this within this young xicanista's soul

See, she reads poem through megaphone
Offering it to those inside
Listening to daughter's heart beat
Through pen and paper

Pleading for mami
Who is locked up away from family
When that is who she was trying to save.

Plucked brows, penciled lips, and scarred truths
    take megaphone now.
This mother, organizer, prisoner once
Now on other side she uses megaphone to tell her vida
Speak for those seen as living dead
But she had forgotten,
Those days of women,
Wounded and weeping.

The women still weep…inside me and you
As a thousand did before me and continue to do

In no-name cell blocks,
Tear-stained kitchens,
And only solace baños

Lagrimas de sangre callendo en las calles de Aztlán
Lagrimas de sangre cayendo en la selva de la realidad

Ya no mas!

See I am haunted,
But I am not scared

As the spirits guide me
Showing me the way of my four mothers
Mujeres en Resistencia
Mujeres en Existencia

Living for those who have come before,
And those yet to come
From the life blood
Of una mujer
Con su luna llena
Vida y muerte dentro de mi
Coyolxauhqui guiandome
En un sacrificio de my own wholey vessel

See, como las mujeres en resistencia
I am willing to shed blood…I do monthly.
Mi sacrificio, my own Xicana powers activating
To give me health and guidance
To allow me to dance with the sun and the moon
En un corrido lleno de pasíon,
Con amor, paz y dignidad.

Tia Chucha
versus
Papa Juan

By Blanca Lutz Banuelos Hernandez

ONE KNEE-HIGH UP, one knee-high down one sunny afternoon standing by the stone pit in the backyard of my childhood home I watched my father stir skillfully over a hot fire the enormous iron skillet where coffee kernels slowly turned from a free green to a dark sticky roasted mass. It was a clear day in all the ways a day could be clear and sunny to a third grader. Dad conversing with me and nudging me to notice his metamorphic concoction, the sun in my hair and knees, the apricot trees abuzz with honey bees behind me and the exuberant smell of caffeine floating in the air all conspired to draw out of me my fiercely guarded dream.

"When I grow up I will be an artist," I heard my voice saying and I saw the words reach Dad's ears—such a simple terrifying statement. I felt my knees buckle as the sun hid behind a cloud; the bees suspended their frenzied honey harvest but the coffee grains sizzled in their terrible dense charcoal black. I fixed my eyes on my chubby hands nervously interlaced in front of me as if trying to grasp back my words and waited for Dad's avalanche… but none came. Instead Dad, with a chuckle, said, "Yes, you will be an artist but spelled with H." Disoriented by his chuckling demeanor I scrambled to mentally spell out artist with H and when I managed it I felt hurt and relieved—hurt that I had not been taken seri-

ously; relieved that I had not been taken seriously. During the early sixties in my natal rural small town in northern Mexico hardworking decent folks considered artistic pursuits the ill-advised occupation of the shiftless, lazy & cunning and females especially suspect of loose morality. An artist (*artista*) spelled with H (*hartista*) comes from the verb "*hartar*" meaning to stuff your mouth or overeat. Thereby, a *hartista* is a glutton.

Papa Juan's comment, although insignificant to him, tainted my creative yearnings with secret shame for many years. Although I delved into several artistic expressions throughout my childhood and well into my thirties, I never quite wore my artistry comfortably and some aspects of it I completely hid for many decades.

Papa Juan was a severe man who prized intellect, hard work… and not much else. All of his children, me included, were routinely the highest achievers in our respective classes. Having been praised and prized for my intellectual achievements for years, I held my heady head as high as my spirit dragged low in sad discontent. It was not that Dad lacked an appreciation for art. To the contrary, our home was always graced with classical music and poetry, but our exposure to art was confined to orthodox, turn of the century European art, heavily

Papa Juan's comment, although insignificant to him, tainted my creative yearnings with secret shame for many years.

worn as the only acceptable expression of proper souls and, of course, useful for intellectual development.

Papa Juan forbade our family to listen, much less enjoy, the populace music or what he termed as "*música de broncos.*" Our little town had one radio station and our radio went dormant exactly at 1 p.m. when the degenerate, disgusting *broncos* would be entertained by the *rancheras* and the *corridos* complete with the "*Ajúas*" y "*Échales.*" As a young child I loved taking my "*Cancionero Picot*" with me up in the trees and singing every raunchy popular song in it. I remember the sweet abandon of making the song mine, even when I did not quite understand every word or sentiment. The song was mine, in my interpretation, in my voice and up in my tree where the wind took it wherever it pleased, hopefully far away from Papa Juan's ears.

During quiet times away from everyone, pen and paper were confidants to my songstress escapades as well as to many other aspects of a less than ideal childhood. Poetry became an easy and comforting confidant. It listened well and it spoke back to me with comfort while promising to keep all my secrets. This was my clandestine artistic world. Publicly, poetry declamation and performance dances for school events were as natural to me as carrying my books to school.

During my teen years fate had me living in Los Angeles and soon after I settled into my previous pattern—accolade geek by day, panting artist after

Writing in secret is an incomplete art, something like the Mona Lisa without the smile—she may be present, but no one shares in her creative joy.

everyone made it to bed. During the decade of my drinking thirties I sang my beloved *broncos'* songs in weekday singing competitions in decaying dives in East LA, where the drink was strong and the competition even stronger. Talented singers would compete for weeks while the cantina broadcasted every Thursday night live on a Mexican radio station. I hardly missed a Thursday some days gathering enough courage from *Don Pedro Domec* to compete myself. I never won but *Pedro Domec* did and I had to quit him along with the Thursday competitions altogether.

I was left with my writing and writing I did. There was so much more material now. Drunks are inquisitive and usually dig in a lot of places sober people are not so easily inclined to dig into. But writing in secret is an incomplete art, something like the Mona Lisa without the smile—she may be present, but no one shares in her creative joy. Having no other public expression of my art, I became increasingly restless. Then around my birthday three years ago I was touched by an urging angel that convinced me I needed to bravely come out

of the shadows by sharing at an open mic.

After some weeks of fighting the winged creature I searched online for open mics within the community. Luis Rodriguez' name came up, a name familiar to me from reading "Always Running." I showed up the first night to open mic at Tia Chucha's not knowing what to expect. What I found was my perching spot in the tall tree of my childhood, a place where I could make my own music, flavor it any way my soul compelled, dressed it in a *bronco* hat or *zapatillas de* ballet, and let it ripple across the vibrating sounds that travelled from my inner most soul to the ears and eyes and souls of other artists like myself. It felt uniting, it felt empowering for when I took my seat among the audience I found myself still on the stage resonating with the words and phrases and cadences of each performer. I found each of them in me and me in them, without the H.

Tia Chucha's uninhibited artistry continues to live among us as a conduit of freedom and healing from the suffocating artistic standards imposed on us by our parents, our cultures, and even ourselves. Tia Chucha's and other likely local open mic places extend an atmosphere where the *bronco* the geek and the all in between can share in the commonality of soul expression that teaches us, nurtures us, grows us, blesses us, and transcends us from the hard and crude experiences of the barrios to the exalted places of the heavenly realms where creating originated and where creation is still first and foremost what makes us human. It is in these creative experiences that we find a commonality that invites the other to a sharing of space and time so contrary to the harsh reality of our barrios where exclusion, seclusion and territorial rivalry are the norm. Where the pressures of living in scarcity of resources pushes us against one another, it is easy to see each other as competitors and even enemies, ah, but where we let our spirits speak through the spirit's own expression in poetry, music, painting, dance, pretend, dream, write, speak, we know who we are and who we are is ONE!

Papa Juan died without knowing his own Tia Chucha and we all lost something precious by his failure to discover his own un-imitated voice. Our *barrios* and the entire world deserve *Que Viva Tia Chucha* in all of us. *Que Viva!!*

La Bamba
A Dream Dance
of Grace

BY RUBÉN "FUNKAHUATL" GUEVARA

**Mural: La Bamba/
Ritchie Valens.
Artist: Hector Ponce.
98 Cent Store,
Pacoima, CA.
Photo: Javier Martinez**

*Para bailar la Bamba, se necesita una poca de gracia, para mi, para ti /
In order to dance The Bamba, you need a little bit of grace, for me, for
you.* So begins La Bamba, a Mexican folk song that became a national hit for Ritchie Valens, a 17-year-old teenager from Pacoima.
Ritchie's meteoric rise to stardom and his tragic death along with La
Bamba's poignant lyrics, serve as a haunting yet inspiring metaphor
for the American Dream and the emerging cultural transformation
of the Northeast San Fernando Valley. Ritchie Valens (aka Ricardo
Estéban Valenzuela Reyes) was a pioneer of Chicano rock and an in-

spiration to many aspiring musicians of Mexican/Latino descent including superstars Santana, Los Lobos, and Los Lonely Boys among many others in the San Fernando Valley, East Los Angeles, and beyond. He was the first American of Mexican heritage to successfully cross over into the rock mainstream at a time when very few had a chance to do so. Ritchie's national hits included La Bamba (#22, 1958), Donna (#2, 1958), Come On Let's Go (#42, 1958), My Little Suzie (#55, 1959), and Little Girl (#92, 1959). His young, prodigious life abruptly ended in a plane crash along with Buddy Holly and J.P "The Big Bopper" Richardson after a concert on February 3, 1959, known as "the day the music died." His former middle school and a local park

Ritchie Valens was a resourceful, self-made musician, even building his own guitars because of lack of funds. This tenacity to pursue a dream against all odds personifies the Mexican American Dream in action.

have been named after him in his honor. He was inducted into the Rock & Roll Hall of Fame in 2001.

Pacoima is a mostly Mexican American working class community in the Northeast San Fernando Valley where Ritchie spent his early childhood and where he developed his astonishing musical talent. He was a resourceful, self-made musician, even building his own guitars because of lack of funds. This tenacity to pursue a dream against all odds personifies the Mexican American Dream in action.

There were other Northeast Valley musicians and bands that attained local and national success such as bandleader Wesley Tuttle Sr. in the 1940s and 50s. Also, The Silhouettes led by Gil Ochoa, a band that Ritchie got his start in. The 1960s brought rock bands The Seeds of Time (with Sylmar High alumnus Johnny Legend), Vito's Classics (winners of many Battle of the Bands in Sylmar), The Tribesmen, Lonnie & The Leg-

ends, and The Du-Vals an R & B band whose leader, bassist, and singer Bill Wild, later became a member of the real Ruben And The Jets, produced by Frank Zappa (1972).

BUT, THE GROUP THAT ATTAINED the greatest national impact after Ritchie (which they were heavily influenced by) were The Innocents from Sun Valley, comprised of members of the car club of the same name. They were Jim West, Darren Stankey, and a Chicano, Al Candelaria, who scored two national hits with *Honest I Do* (#28, 1960), *Gee Whiz* (#28, 1961), and backed Kathy Young's *A Thousand Stars* (#3, 1960). They toured nationally with Allan Freed's road show along with stars Jerry Lee Lewis, The Shirelles, Etta James, and Chubby Checker. Just kids with a love of music and the ambition to pursue a dream against all odds—and they were formidable odds.

That tenacious dream and legacy has endured into the 21st century inspiring conscious Hip Hop groups such as Aztlán Underground (Yaotl, Bean, Zorock, Peps) and El Vuh (Victor-E, Zero, E-Rise) among others to write and record songs about indigenous rights and identity as well as social injustice, which the Northeast Valley has unfortunately been guilty of. In 1992, the notorious brutal beating of African American Rodney King by the Los Angeles Police Department in Lake View Terrace ignited the L.A. uprising. Unfortunately, there has been a long history of unchecked and unwarranted confrontation between the police and Valley residents of color going back many decades.

There has also been a long history of a lack of cultural centers for youth to develop as artists—musicians, writers, painters, dancers, and actors—until Tía Chucha's Centro Cultural & Bookstore arrived in Sylmar in 2001. A safe cultural oasis emerged offering an opportunity to cultivate future artists as well as a community forum for relevant discussion and action.

Finally, the Northeast San Fernando Valley and beyond can now dance the lyrics to *La Bamba* with firm gentle grace while dreaming and turning into reality a brighter future for the arts and the community. Would've made Ritchie happy and proud.

Recuerdos de Sylmar
Cholos, Punks, and Xicana/o Revolutionary Consciousness

By Yaotl Mazahua,
LEAD SINGER OF AZTLÁN UNDERGROUND
As told to Denise M. Sandoval

We didn't cross the borders, the borders crossed us! Yet the settler nation lives in disgust! The American dream only for some Play the role and forget where you came from.

("Decolonize," 1998)

MY NAME IS YAOTL MAZAHUA, but I was born Rene Leonard Orozco in the San Fernando Valley. I was born on Mott Street in 1965. I have lived for 46 years in Sylmar and I am father of four children. I grew up in Sylmar, and where I grew up there were a lot of people from Oklahoma and Arkansas who came in the 1930s because this area used to be all agriculture, like lemons, oranges and olives. It was a very polemic time because I had racial experiences in elementary school and junior high in Sylmar. When I was in second grade I would be walking from my home to El Dorado Elementary School. There would be these "hicks" and they would call me "beaner" and "wetback." Many times they would beat me up. Even in school I had teachers who were from Kentucky and they would make anti-Mexican remarks. I had that vibe like "we don't belong." I was a "latchkey kid" because my mom worked like from 3 pm to 11 pm and my dad worked from 6 pm to 3 am. And so when I transferred from elementary to junior high, I ended up joining a gang because of the racial tensions.

Iconoclast, circa 1983. Photo courtesy of Yaotl Mazahua.

Aztlán Underground.
Photo:
Javier Martinez

One of the lures of joining a gang is you didn't have to get beaten up anymore. I remember my art teacher saying "wetback" like this was nothing. During that time we would go to the market and my dad would speak to me in Spanish and I'd be like "shut up." I'd be really ashamed. At that time *cholos* didn't actually shave their heads. I think punks later inspired the shaved heads for *cholos*. Back then you'd comb your hair back, wear a white T-shirt, khaki pants, and bandannas. I started wearing that style in middle school, in seventh grade. Then I almost died when I was in the eighth grade because I was going up the ranks in the gang. I got jumped into *San Fer Pee Wee Locos*—this was like the junior gang of San Fernando. San Fernando and Sylmar were considered the same territory. When I got jumped in, I tried to go up the ranks. My way of going up the ranks was to out-drink everyone. I tried to out-drink the leader and it got crazy. I got alcohol poisoning and almost died. Around ninth grade or tenth grade, I still had a sense of rebellion. For me being a gangster or a *cholo* was a sense of "F-U," a sense of empower-

ment. I'm not going to lie—I felt neglected at home. I mean my parents fed me, but I didn't have the emotional support.

Then I see these people with shaved heads at my school. Some of them were brown. I heard, "Oh it's a punk band man, you should check it out." So I went there and there was this sense of nihilism, a sense of rebellion. The lyrics and the music was like "I'm about to have a nervous breakdown," things that were angry, and I identified with that. But the music also had a sense of consciousness. There was a critical analysis of society, of the power structure and of class. Some of the bands that influenced me were *The Stains* out of East Los Angeles, a *cholo*-punk band. Also *Southern Death Cult* from England that included an indigenous worldview in their music. There was a lot of empowerment there. This was an education for me, a sense of being. This was a place where I belonged in the world. This was happening in L.A.

There was a club out here called "Godzilla's" in Sun Valley in the early 1980s. There was a little punk scene here in Sylmar, and they included brown and white. In a way this was the antithesis of the racial tension I grew up with. At the same time there was no sense of being Mexican. I became intensively active in the punk scene from 1980 to 1985. I was in two bands *Iconoclast* (1981 to 1985) and *The Wankers* (1985 to 1986). Music saved my life; it shaped the future direction of my life.

You try to be white and it's very respectable/But be Xicano and its highly unacceptable. Then we're termed Hispanic as if we were from Spain/Trying to insert us in the American game/And we're called wetbacks like we've never been here/When our existence on this continent is thousands of years/This is the state of the indigena *today.*
(Decolonize, 1998)

I was also hanging out in Hollywood and I came across this flyer. It said *Four Directions*, Aztec dancers, and Native American poet/activist John Trudell. I saw the dancers. I heard John Trudell—it was heavy stuff. I joined a dance group and they gave me a lot of knowledge of indigenous consciousness. They were the only Aztec dance group in all of Los Angeles at that time. If anything the music of art, the sharing and the communication that art has like music, became medicine for me. It was a sense of identity. It brought me back to who I am, and it built me. That's why the seeds for creating *Aztlán Underground* began in 1988; the band was fully realized by 1990. By this time, I had gone through a personal self-discovery—feeling ostracized, like I didn't belong, and my people not having a sense of identity. Many people think being Mexican is just speaking Spanish—our culture goes beyond that. It's deeper. We had a song with lyrics that said, "I'm not Hispanic/*Yo soy Chicano/Yo soy indigena/ No soy Hispano/ Con pura sangre Mexicano*." It was all identity politics. We were going to lay it down, bridge the instruments that we learned in *danza* and bring it with hip-hop as a platform. Our whole thing was trying to empower people so they'd know they had a past, although it was unfamiliar to them—we can't have a future without understanding our past.

IN 1996, ZACK DE LA ROCHA of Rage Against the Machine organized an *Encuentro* with the Zapatistas in Chiapas. One of the messages that the Zapatistas espoused was if you're a writer, write; if you're a musician, make music; if you're an organizer, organize; if you're a mother raise your kids. Everyone has a place in raising consciousness and bringing out the dialogue for change, to do this together. There's a difference between being a revolutionary and being a rebel. We're not about assuming power—we're about what do the people want. So one of the things that we said when we came back was "you have to ask the people what they want." The Zapatistas call this *Consultas*. We did surveys. We would stand on the streets, mostly in East Los Angeles and the San Fernando Mall. We asked people, "Hey what's going on or what are your concerns?" And their concerns were about graffiti, gangs, drugs. That was the idea: You ask people what their concerns were, and the people tell you.

As humanity, we all need healing in one way or another. This is medicine. The arts are medicine that is neglected many times, although the arts could lead to profound movements as shown throughout history. When Tia Chucha's opened up it was like a flower in a desert, like there's actually a place where people can dialogue and learn from each other—and from the perspective of "art as the catalyst." This is the place where people can have an opportunity to grow. The arts play an important role in bettering our communities. Today *Aztlán Underground* recently celebrated their 20th Anniversary and is in this place where we want to create stories, not only with our music, but multimedia. We

As humanity, we all need healing in one way or another. This is medicine. The arts are medicine that is neglected many times, although the arts could lead to profound movements as shown throughout history.

are interested in the human condition—such as mental health, sexuality, and our own inner struggles. These are part of our own consciousness even in terms of being a good organizer. We have to have good mental health to be good parents, brothers, sisters, and organizers. We have to be in tune with ourselves to make a firm impact, to get where we are trying to get to "as a people." We're trying to show how art is medicine and that it's a catalyst for change.

To the earth, to the air, to the fire, and to the water/The eagle and condor have met/We must realize/Our connection to this land
(Decolonize, 1998)

Policy
of Sweet
Bread
for the
Hungry Heart

By Matriz

asked to voice our knots, display our tangles,
present them in beauty, fit for the public,
a contradiction, a delicate artful challenge
thus this attempt, holding close the interest of we

bombarded by so much sensation, news of abuse
shooters erupt, thirst blazing, wrinkled with fears,
uterus empty of mothering, broken warriors gone wild,
loss felling children, uniformed walls,
    all distant relatives

tired, bones witness the gathering day workers storm
weary, business suits fit to neglect needs,
angry, skeletons fed on promises of better tomorrows,
self-medicated, sick of bankruptcies, graduation job lies

the marchers emerge, demanding rights
to knowledge, to health, to be spectators no more,
pledging our world to transform, for worth
    in *this* lifetime,
together pounding the pavement, lifting spirits
    to the sky

listen to the prayer of a nation humbled by mistakes,
embrace and brace for changes, expect this
    once and for all,
rely on the wealth of the creative, let it flow
    into every gap,
reject addictions rooted in usurped authority,
    robbed power

Mother Earth waits for her children to
    grasp their lesson
that there are natural laws greater than
    the games of man
that a well being is measured by dignity beyond its own
that the abundance we seek is already in our midst,

so be wise, responsive: there's only enough time to align

Random
Flow

BY AARON CASTELLANOS

Mile after mile, the strips of concrete that run along the Yellow,

The Yellow of the sun, that shines in my window and blinds my Eyes,

These Eyes that have seen my people struggle for a life that's Free,

Free like the air that I breathe in, wandering like the birds that Fly,

Fly high above our foreheads, migrating in a single unit like a Family,

My Family, whom I miss deeply, my support through my Education,

The Education an AB540 student fights for everyday in the Classroom,

The same Classroom of half-filled minds being taught by Revolutionaries,

The educational Guerrilla Fighters in suits and designer Jeans,

Those blue Jeans we wear, made from sweatshop labor in the Far East,

But how Far East do we have to go, to find pain, to find Corruption,

Corrupted government officials in slave America and in drug-infested Mexico,

Beloved Mexico, filled with memories and a dark history of Massacres,

Indigenous Massacres, student massacres that we remember the 2nd of October,

October, the month I was born, situated in the middle of a beautiful Sunset,

The same Sunset that strikes the trees as they glow red, the leaves as they Fall,

But it's those hands that Fall into the soil and come back up with Tomatoes,

Tomatoes picked by my brothers and sisters, colored martyrs of warm Blood,

The same Blood that runs through our veins, runs through my Heart,

My Heart which I'm still trying to learn from, listen from, Feel from,

I'm Feeling the weight of choices and predicaments that congest my Body,

Oh how my Body aches, from drinking that cheap vodka last Night,

Night after night, how I stare at the photos of the past, far now Away,

And I'm far Away, something I'm still trying to cope with, grasp ever so Hard,

I wonder how Hard that car crash felt, after that drunk driver ran the red Light,

I wake up to red Lights, illuminating the numbers that measure the flow of Motion,

The same Motion we ignore, the rotation of mother Earth,

Filled with oceans of blue and lands of green, she's not satisfied, not Happy,

The same unHappiness she felt as she sat there waiting for a phone Call that never came,

I should have Called her back, but I didn't, I went to bed underneath cotton Sheets,

I need to wash those Sheets, twisting dynamics of daily Routines,

It's the Routine I need to break from, the habit that seems to control my Driving,

I'm Driving far, coming back home to where my heart is, the beautiful Valley,

Oh how I miss the Valley, floating clouds of music that whistles in the Wind,

The Wind blows, passes me by, just like all those iron birds on the Freeway,

I live on the Freeway, continuously traveling because that's what humans do,

I need to move, I can't stay here, I'm being sucked back into this Void,

The Void which I'm struggling to fill, everyone has their own Struggles,

So many Fights for the right of equality, for justice, for outside ears to Listen,

Listen... what do you hear? There's no Talking,

Because people feel awkward with silence, so they talk, and that's the problem,

Everyone's Talking and no one is listening to each Other,

Tell the Others to wait, let's start walking, taking the first step of a Journey,

Where's the next Journey? I hope it's not artificial like what I'm Buying,

I'm Buying in, into my soul, I'm learning its language, I hope it's not too Late.

La **Paleta**

BY CEASAR AVELAR

(Dedicated to all parents and children around the world who find themselves trapped in poverty)

So this is it?

This is what my future is all about?

An eternity of being poor

A lifetime of being imprisoned by my own lack
    of financial means

Even an ugly day is beautiful when you have money
Children from the neighborhood run to their parents
When the *paletero* man (ice cream man) yells

Paletas!

Paletas!

But not my son

At least not today

Today we had to watch Sesame Street with
    the volume up at full blast

Just so we wouldn't have to hear the enticing yells of

Raspados!
Elotes!
Paletas!

His cries shake the inner fibers of my soul

His sadness cuts deep and beyond the scar tissue
    of my identity

So now what?

Now what Uncle Sam?

You got me cornered and my heart just won't let me
    call it quits

You take away jobs
I find ways to get money
You raise tuition and I find ways to obtain an education

My back is wet because you've soaked it in stigma
You keep punching and I move forward
You give me your best shot and still can't seem
    to put me down

Without any money all I can do is

Think
Read
And dream

And I've come to the conclusion that
    you owe us a future

And my son an ice cream

Si Se Puede. 14x17
Oil on Canvas. 2008.
Artist: Erica Friend.
Sylmar, CA.

When Butterflies Soar Free | A Monarca in Resistance

By KARINA CEJA

LIKE THE MONARCH BUTTERFLY that journeys for survival across Turtle Island, a two-spirit monarch migrated north from the beautiful state of Michoacan, México to Tongva/Tataviam land seeking better opportunities. At two years of age, this P'urhépecha (*Purépecha*) blood left her cocoon behind to trek the Sonoran desert and cross man-made borders by her mother's hand to finally arrive in the urban city of Pacoima, in the San Fernando Valley. This new land, culture, and society were to become her home away from home. As the oldest sibling and only daughter, I learned to create my own path as a struggling Chicanita by reclaiming my existence, owning my identity, and acting on it.

I remember as soon as I could speak English, my very first job became as an interpreter for my parents. My role was to translate letters, applications, school forms, and conversations. As a result, the direct participation in my families' life and surroundings led to my exposure and awareness of the real struggles communities of color face while in search of "better opportunity." I began to question why we didn't have certain commodities, or weren't able to return to Mexico to visit my Grandma. I rejected the status quo even before I knew it existed. I was a feminist before I was able to theorize it. I challenged gender and sexuality as a tomboy fighting for space amongst the boys. I stood up to sexism by standing up to my father's machismo. I resisted against the statistics that hovered over me as a brown-skinned girl in the hood, growing up as an undocumented youth, among gang violence, teen pregnancy and limited resources. Witnessing my friends fall through the cracks of a broken educational system, the odds of succeeding were few. I searched for an outlet and began to explore the shelved walls of Pacoima Branch Library. Only a block away from home, Pacoima library became a sanctuary where I practiced my reading skills, learned to use computers, and discovered the Internet—a place that opened my mind to worlds that existed outside of my own. Full of hope and self-determination, I continued on a path towards higher education, a path I felt would honor the journey my parents trekked to provide me and my brothers with a more dignified future.

FAST FORWARD TO 2001. I was a recent high school graduate and soon to become the first in my entire family to attend a university. As a rebel monarca always flying against the currents of the wind, I was determined to challenge the male-dominated science careers and majored in computer engineering. There, students were individualistic, competitive and had no sense of support for one another, especially for a young womyn of color. It wasn't long before I took my first Chicana/o Studies class and instantly had a change of heart. This was the first time my ideas, anger, and existence were legitimized in an empowering way. The love and support was like nothing I had felt in my first two years of college. Without a doubt I changed my major and soon after joined Movimiento Estudiantil Chicana/o de Aztlan (M.E.Ch.A.), where I began to develop my political identity. M.E.Ch.A. was my stepping-stone to better conceptualize my struggle, and where I developed a passion for activism making a lifetime commitment to community-oriented work.

A year after graduation, the universe and a good friend brought me to the doors of the only cultural center in the San Fernando Valley, Tia Chucha's Centro Cultural & Bookstore. The centro and I had an instant connection. I came in to drop off my resume and I left for home as the new Music LA! program coordinator. I was thrilled. This immediately became more than a job, this was the perfect opportunity to practice accountability with the community that raised me. At Tia Chucha's, I learned to work in a holistic environment among a group of compassionate and spiritually driven individuals, all committed to servicing disenfranchised communities.

Advocating on behalf of the arts, literacy, and cultura, I transitioned to the program coordinator of the centro, a position that gave me full creative direction of the programs and events at Tia Chucha's. Tia Chucha's plays an important role in my life because it was the catalyst of my organizing experience outside the academic institution. For three years, it taught me the meaning of commitment and witnessed the importance of creativity and the arts as transformational mediums for youth and families. I always saw myself working at Tia Chucha's for a very long time. I was committed to its vision and had established meaningful relationships with the staff and supporters. I had built another family. While at an encampment to save a sacred mountain in Arizona, I received a vision from the universe. I realized the im-

I stood up to sexism by standing up to my father's machismo. I resisted against the statistics that hovered over me as a brown-skinned girl in the hood, growing up as an undocumented youth, among gang violence, teen pregnancy and limited resources.

portance and recognized the urgency of actualizing my own ideas and visions within my community of Pacoima. Trusting in my heart that I was making the right decision, I began an emotional yet peaceful process of transitioning out of Tia Chucha's, constantly reminding myself that this was simply another change in my relationship with the centro. This was my transition from employee into a lifetime commitment of solidarity work as a supporter of this cultural oasis.

While I was still working at Tia Chucha's, I had moved into a collective home with a group of like-minded individuals interested in working towards building a community of radical thinkers and doers to prefigure the just and dignified world humyns should live in. This meant that we would live in our home the way we wished to live in the world. The first six months we focused on building a strong foundation, by creating a collective vision and developing healthy interpersonal relationships amongst the six housemates. During this process we learned of each other's politics, understood our intersectionalities, embraced our strengths and found ways to make up for each other's shortcomings. We established collectivity, communication, and respect as our most fundamental agreements; inspired by the organized work of ants each of our "I's" became "we" and together we moved forward as El Hormiguero ("the ant hill").

El Hormiguero is both a home and a communal space, a resource for the community. We hope to inspire through our actions a different way of living with each other and the earth. As a collective home, we distribute cleaning duties every week, we buy food together, and split the bills and general expenses. We have weekly meetings where we elaborate on our home and our projects as a way to keep us consistent and effective,

El Hormiguero is both a home and a communal space, a resource for the community. We hope to inspire through our actions a different way of living with each other and the earth.

but most importantly, accountable to our work. We believe in food-sovereignty, that food is a humyn right, that land belongs to those who work it and that mother earth is our collective responsibility. Following the ways of our ancestors, we grow our own food. Some of us are better farmers than others, but together we cultivate a healthy garden that feeds and sustains us.

As a community space we believe knowledge and information should be shared through an anti-capitalist way—an each-one teach-one environment without capital exchange. We created "The Berry: Center for Research and Knowledge Enhancement," a lending library with a collection of some of our favorite books. We also added "La Otra Berry," a knowledge and information distribution center where people can share zines, newsletters, pamphlets, and local event flyers. Both of these projects intend to provide readily available information and function as a resource for the community. We believe that education is a right and should be free to all that seek it.

TEATRO INTERGALACTICO 3001, aside from the funky name, is simply our newly recreated living room into a multi-use space. We host film nights and provide a space for dialogue and discussion. El Teatro Intergalactico 3001 is also a meeting space for other groups, like the San Fernando Valley Dream Team and the Young Warriors. It is a reliable space for healing and talking circles like our Queer Healing Oasis. The Queer Healing Oasis is a safe, vibrant, and positive environment for Queer and ally people of color that promotes personal growth, healing, and wellness. Spaces that cater to Queer people of color seldom sprout in our communities, therefore it is up to us to plant those seeds and nurture them.

However, the most established of all is our garage, the home base of Bikesan@s del Valle and it's bicycle cooperative. Bikesan@s del Valle is a collective of cyclists that focus on sharing bike mechanic skills, cyclist rights information, and redistribute used bikes for people in need. The co-op works on a mutual aid basis, meaning we do not charge for the services we simply ask for reciprocity in diverse ways of support and solidarity. If monetary donations are made we make sure to not compromise our autonomy or self-sustainability. Bikesana/os derived its name from paisana/o, a term of endearment among people from the same geographical area. We mainly serve the Spanish-speaking undocumented and working class community of Pacoima, considering 33 percent of its residents use a bicycle as their

main mode of transportation, many because they are denied access to driver's licenses. As a result, Bikesan@s seeks to foster a cyclist-friendly atmosphere and inspire a conscious, healthy, and self-reliable community on wheels.

ASPIRING TO BE THE MAIN ARTERY of information at El Hormiguero, *La Hormiga*, a newsletter and online media project written by the community and for the community, aims to cultivate seeds of knowledge, resistance, and liberation in the midst of corporate media manipulations. La Hormiga intends to develop trust and loyalty within the local community to provide them with real news and information in order to reclaim media that is directly affecting us, while also highlighting the creative and alternative methods our communities develop to function within this unjust system. With the online media project our opportunities are endless. We plan to create audio and video outlets that will focus on local issues but always retaining the connection to broader injustices that affect us all globally. We believe that a well-informed community is the biggest threat to an oppressive system and in the midst

of budget cuts to many educational sectors, it is time to recreate the way we teach, learn and exchange knowledge with each other.

Even though El Hormiguero is still a seedling, we feel our roots get deeper and stronger with the work we have done thus far. We recognize that we have a lot of work ahead and we are intensely committed to a decolonized and transformative way of living, relating, and organizing that incites true change in the hearts, minds, and spirits of communities in struggle. We will continue to work towards dismantling all the "isms" that oppress, remembering that if one person is not free, none of us are free. Through dialogue, mutual aid, and horizontal power we can reclaim our streets and livelihood block-by-block to recreate our paths and align them with the ways of our ancestors. Only collectively can we be the change we need in the world and El Hormiguero believes that not only is another world possible, it is under construction.

Now this two-spirited monarca—embodying both masculine and feminine energies—metamorphosized into a balanced way of being both butterfly and ant, the balance between the earth and the sky.

A Barrio Playground
Urban Street Skateboarding in Pacoima

By Angel F. Hernandez

Skater Martin Yañez at Prod Skate Plaza. Photo: Giovanni Darkins

AT THE CORNER of Laurel Canyon Blvd and Paxton Street lies one of the most important youth spaces in Pacoima. This space is known as the Ritchie Valens Recreation Center. It consists of an indoor gymnasium, a soccer field, outdoor basketball courts, a jungle gym, a baseball diamond, as well as handball and tennis courts. However, these amenities are not the main attraction. Its secret weapon is actually located to the left of the tennis courts. It is known as the Paul Rodriguez Skate Plaza. This is a "free of charge" skate park that was envisioned by professional skateboarder Paul Rodriguez Jr. aka PRod, LA 84 Foundation, and the Nike SB (skateboarding) line of Nike, Inc. Since its inception this space has become an urban paradise that young brown bodies use to claim an identity and build community by utilizing the skateboard as their medium of self-expression.

The nuances pertaining to spatial relations, urban-street skateboarding, and the Pacoima youth are vital factors to examine. Urban-public space is both the context and the product of material and "symbolic social relationships," and thus connected to identity formation. More specifically, skateboarders often formulate their identity as a specific "kind" of skater based on what type of spaces are accessible to them. Were this space not available to these youth, they would perhaps actualize their potentiality of engaging in other mundane and stereotypical activities of *barrio* life such as gangs, drugs, loitering, etc.

Class dynamics are also embedded within the two main styles of skateboarding: vert and street. Vert (vertical) skateboarding is widely recognized as skateboarding on ramps, half-pipes, bowls, pools, and is mostly available in big skate parks that typically charge entry fees and are usually located in more affluent privatized areas. The more accessible style of skateboarding, and the most practiced of either form, is street skateboarding. It consists of skating on ledges, rails, benches, K-12 public school tables, loading docks, stair-sets, etc. Urban-street skateboarding as a form of self- expression is available to all—however, skateboarders who are of lower socio-economic status overpopulate it. That is why this park is so important—it is located in a disenfranchised neighborhood and specifically caters to urban street-skateboarders based on its architecture.

THE PAUL RODRIGUEZ SKATE PLAZA is no conventional skate park. It is a skate park designed to meet the specific needs of urban street-skateboarders. After the end of the golden era of skateboarding during the late 70s and early 80s, skate parks were virtually terminated due to liability and insurance concerns. Skateboarders no longer had ample access to vert skating and therefore decided to hit the streets more aggressively. This was essentially where the idea of an urban street-skateboarder was conceived. The PRod Skate Plaza is thus a testament to this genealogy of skateboarding's history and evolution. It is not filled with ramps, bowls, quarter pipes, etc. Rather, it was built based on actual skateboarding locations around the city of Los Angeles. At the main entrance one is greeted by what appears to be a broken yellow barricade. But this is merely a facade representative of the relationship that exists between skateboarding and the law; skateboarding is forbidden and criminalized in many spaces around Los Angeles and greater Los Angeles.

As one skates through the park, the first "spot" that one encounters is a small transition skateboarding area that then leads to four ledges, placing you at the center of the park consisting of a stage that hosts a "Sylmar 9" replica (a stair set located in Sylmar High School that was popularized by PRod in the skateboarding video *Forecast*). These unique characteristics remind the skateboarders that the park is a world within itself. A world they partake in, contribute to and inhabit. It is very common to find anywhere from 20-40 young men hanging out and skateboarding in this skate plaza.

In an interview with local skateboarder Robert Coloma, aka "Diddy," age 14, he stated that his favorite "spot" to skate was the "9 rail" (Symar 9 Replica). This is where he spends much of his spare time perfecting his tricks in hopes of receiving sponsorship. Sponsorship can be an avenue to class mobility for many skateboarders. It also influences the practice of skateboarding in urban settings, transforming itself from an everyday activity to possibly a career because it demands hard work and dedication. The school system in the Northeast San Fernando Valley has created a sense of disconnection and isolation, therefore education is not viewed as a viable means of attaining class mobility. Diddy echoes this fact when he states that at San Fernando High School, "no one goes to class, like half of the school doesn't go to class... they just kick it there and ditch, they don't even drop out." He also informed me that he was grateful for the space that the skate plaza provides when he asserts, "I can't see myself doing anything else besides this. I suck at everything else, but I'm really good at skating."

For me growing up in L.A. skateboarding was like that's the place, if you wanna be a skater that's the place you wanna grow up—it's L.A. I definitely think it's kept a lot of kids out of trouble... a lot of kids who would normally be up to no good.

—*Paul Rodriguez Jr. (December 9, 2010)*

Other skateboarders also perfect their craft here and are engaged in the urban street-skateboarding lifestyle. Local skateboarder Jonathan Hernandez, age 17, spoke to the necessity of alternative urban-public spaces: "There are neighborhoods that need them [skate parks] more than others, cus it keeps us away from doing stuff like drugs, maybe gang-banging, you know, it keeps us busy." Upon engaging in this ethnographic work, I became aware of the reality that for many of these youth, skateboarding is one of the very few alternative recre-

Skater Angel Victor Hernandez. Photo: Giovanni Darkins

ational options available to them that they find appealing. Street-skateboarding has been dubbed a rebel culture by mainstream accounts. Notwithstanding, the skateboarders at PRod's park are evidence that rebel cultures are thriving in public spaces, engaged in building community, while negotiating identity through an alternative lifestyle like street-skateboarding.

Tony Avalos, age 23, provided some great insight in regards to the community prior to the building of the park. He stated, "It's cleared up a lot, it's getting better from when I was growing up to now—it's cleaned up a lot. I think it's a good thing that they built this here, because I've seen a lot of kids just get better at skating,

> ## Skateboarding changes a lot of people's lives, it changed my life for the most part. I've met people I probably would have never met if I didn't step on a skateboard.
>
> —*Thomas Ortiz*

you know, versus being in gangs and out in the street. Like I see a lot of kids just focusing on skating."

There existed a consensus among the interviewees that the Paul Rodriguez Skate Plaza was beneficial to this community. It essentially serves as a safe haven for

this urban street-skateboarding cultural milieu. Nonetheless, we must be reminded that though this space exists, there is also a constant battle occurring between skateboarders and the law. The animosity that exists between skateboarders and the law is quite prevalent in urban settings, and the Northeast San Fernando Valley is no exception.

During our interview, Diddy informed me that the cops in San Fernando were more repressive than in Pacoima: "We were right there [skateboarding] at San Fernando middle school, the cops got us, and they gave us all tickets." He told me they were fined $1,000 each for trespassing into state government property; there were eight of them in total. These youth do not have the means to pay these fees, which means they can potentially face jail time, all for the act of skateboarding. The *hypercriminalization* of inner-city youth, particularly youth of color, is rampant. As defined by urban ethnographer Victor Rios, *hypercriminalization* is the process by which an individual's everyday behaviors and styles become ubiquitously treated as deviant, risky, threatening, or criminal, across social contexts.

THE RELATIONSHIP BETWEEN skateboarding and the law is one of peculiarity. But not in this space—the only laws that are broken here are the laws of gravity. As these skaters perform their tricks down the "Sylmar 9" replica stair set, they accomplish far more than landing a complex aerial maneuver vis-à-vis their skateboard. They are also gaining confidence, intrinsic motivation, and bonding. Furthermore, they are building community, this can be observed when they are embraced by their other skater *homies* for landing a difficult trick, or when they motivate one another to continue to practice a trick until they land it successfully. Thomas Ortiz stated that *Pacas* (Pacoima) has "always been a big skate community, but with the building of this plaza, it just helped bring them all together at once. I mean you would see them here and there, down the street, just, like, 'oh look it's another person on a skateboard.' But when you start coming here, at least four times a week like I do, you start recognizing people, like 'oh hey dude, I know you, what's your name?' and that's how you make friends..." The skaters at the PRod Skate Plaza did not see themselves only as individuals but also as a part of a bigger family, their skate family.

The predominant sentiment of interviewed skateboarders was that skateboarding is far more than a hobby—to them it is a lifestyle. Every lifestyle needs a space in which to thrive and visualize full potentiality. The free of charge, free of criminalization space that the Paul Rodriguez Skate Plaza provides is indeed a safe-haven for the youth in Pacoima. Skateboarding in this *barrio* has become an alternative form of social resistance in which these young [brown] men build community and re-negotiate identity. As urban spaces evolve in the Northeast San Fernando Valley, the effects of a neoliberal conception of the city will remain a matter of debate. The issue becomes even more problematic when urban development in the form of attracting major corporations takes precedence over investments in youth services such as community centers, art programs, skate-parks, etc. For some, urban street-skateboarding is just another sport. But for the youth who utilize the public space that the Paul Rodriguez Skate Plaza provides, skateboarding has in fact been a nurturing oasis within the harsh reality of the privatization of public space, the criminalization of alternative youth cultures, and post-industrial decay. More efforts for public spaces like the PRod Skate Park are essential for the cultural survival of urban youth.

I am René, the Boy
Soy René, el niño

By René Colato Laínez

7-11 Mural.
Sylmar, CA.
Photo:
Javier Martinez

MY NAME IS RENÉ, like my grandfather and my father. I am René, the third. I learned to write my name in El Salvador. I wrote it everywhere. I wrote it with the charcoal from Mamá's brick oven. I traced it with a stick on the fresh rained soil. In El Salvador, I was René the brave, René the strong and René the funny. I cannot believe it. Here, in the United States, René is a girl's name!

I DISCOVERED IT when a new student joined my classroom and Miss Soria called roll.

"José, Mary, Carlos."

"Here," answered everyone.

"René," she said.

As I started to say "here" with pride, I heard a girl's voice answer to my name. She was the new student.

"Here I am. I'm Renee!" she said.

She looked at me and smiled. My mouth dropped. I was paralyzed.

During recess, some boys came up and taunted me, "You have a girl's name!"

IN THE KITCHEN, while we were eating fried plantains with sour cream and hot chocolate, I told my parents, "The boys at school say that René is a girl's name."

I have never heard such a thing," Papá said. "René is the name of hard-working men."

"René is a beautiful name. Don't listen to them," Mamá said.

"That's right, my name is so beautiful that a girl copied it from me!" I said as a piece of fried plantain disappeared into my mouth.

René Has Two Last Names | René tiene dos apellidos

BY RENÉ COLATO LAÍNEZ

ON THE FIRST DAY at my new school, my teacher, Miss Soria, gave me a sticker that said René Colato. The sticker was missing my second last name. Maybe Miss Soria's pen ran out of ink. I took my pencil and added it. Now it looked right: René Colato Laínez.

IN EL SALVADOR, I wrote my name on my homework, my books, and my birthday party invitations. René Colato Laínez was a happy song that made me dance to the rhythms of the cha cha cha. But in the United States, the song lost the güiros, maracas and drums. Why does my name have to be different here?

AT MY DESK, I wrote my name on a piece of paper. When I wrote Colato, I saw my grandparents René and Amelia singing with me. When I wrote Laínez, I saw my grandparents Ángela and Julio dancing with me. René Colato looked incomplete. It was like a hamburger without the meat or a pizza without cheese or a hot dog without a wiener. Yuck!

La Guayaba Kitchen
Creating Community through Food

We see food as a revolution, as a way to claim our space in the culinary world while staying true to our roots.

—*La Guayaba Kitchen*

Wendee Pizano is originally from Pacoima and currently resides in Sylmar. She is the founder and executive chef of La Guayaba Kitchen, a small catering business that also offers cooking workshops to the community. Her interest in food began at an early age while watching her mom and tias cook and gather the family for dinner. She always thought there was something special and intriguing about cooking and sharing food with loved ones. As she grew older, her interest in food increased as she sought to reconnect with the foods of her grandmothers and tias-abuelas.

THE PURPOSE of La Guayaba Kitchen is to recreate the recipes we as Chicanas/os grew up eating at home and to also share memories/experiences connected through food. La Guayaba Kitchen in no means claims to be 100 percent Mexican food though. This organization is made up of Chicana home cooks and its food reflects experiences as residents in the Northeast San Fernando Valley. Guayaba Kitchen's food is a mixture of what one grew up eating with family and the unique gastronomy experiences encountered here in the Southwest.

Guayaba Kitchen sees food as a revolution, as a way to claim a spot in the culinary world while staying true to their Mexican/ Chicana/o roots. Guayaba Kitchen also offers vegetarian and vegan foods, menu planning, catering, and personal chef services. Guayaba Kitchen's blog is updated with recipes, pictures, and rants daily. For more information, please check out: www.guayabakitchen.com/

Lupe's Beer-Battered
Fish Tacos

MY ELDEST SISTER LUPE is a great cook. She was born and raised in Mexico and had the opportunity to cook alongside aunts, grandmas, and other señoras in the rancho. Even though she has been in this country for about 20 years, she has not lost her *sazon*! My sister and her family live far from L.A., but they come a couple of times a year and we do what we do best: Feast! Last time she came, she made beer battered fish tacos and they were bomb! Here is my version of her recipe! Enjoy!

P.S. For you vegetarians out there, substitute fish with thick slices of Portobello mushrooms!

Ingredients:
oil for frying
5 Tilapia fillets
Salt & Pepper to taste
pinch of smoked paprika
for batter
1 ½ cup all purpose flour
1 tsp sea salt
1tsp cracked pepper
1 tsp garlic powder
½ tsp dried oregano
½ bottle of pale ale beer
(I use *Rolling Rock,* but *Corona* works well too)
1 ½ tbsp spicy brown mustard

How to prepare:
Heat 2 inches of oil in skillet over moderate heat while you prepare the fish and batter.

Cut fillets in half lengthwise to create 2 strips. Season strips with salt and pepper to taste and add a pinch of smoked paprika. Set aside while you make the batter.

For batter: In a mixing bowl add all dry ingredients and mix to incorporate. Slowly whisk in the beer. Avoid adding beer all at once because it will create lumps. If mixture is too dry, add more beer. Batter should be a little runnier than pancake batter. Whisk until all lumps are gone, then mix in mustard. Don't worry if there is a lump here or there.

Once the oil is hot, dip a strip into the batter, allow some of the batter to drip off, and place in hot oil. Add only about 3 strips per batch to ensure proper cooking. Fry for 4 minutes on each side or until golden brown. Set aside fried fish on a paper lined dish to drain. Continue with the remaining strips.

Roughly chop fried fillets and set aside (1 fillet (2 strips) will make 3 tacos). Heat tortillas on comal and stuff with chopped fried fish. Top with purple cabbage and our cilantro habañero crema (available at www.guayabakitchen.com).Serve with a lime wedge and fresh radishes!

Makes 12-15 tacos (suggested service size: 3 tacos)

The Evolution of a
Revolutionary

BY JENNIFER "JENUINE" ALUMBAUGH

I stepped inside with a quiet reverence about my soul, for this was no ordinary place.

"THIS IS TIA CHUCHA'S, you in the right place?" he said as he walked toward the doorway from the table where he had been sitting. Tattoos rippled over the rich brown canvas of his arms as they flexed and rested, folded over his chest. He was waiting for my answer.

"I'm here for open mic?" I said, more of a question than a statement.

He looked me up and down and I prepared myself for him to give me directions back to the highway and send me along my way when instead he nodded in recognition, moved aside, and opened the door for me.

I stepped inside with a quiet reverence about my soul for this was no ordinary place. This was no run-of-the-mill, one-in-every-plaza chain bookstore. No. This is a sacred space, the fruit of a toilsome labor, the offspring of a dream conceived and long carried; the kind of space that inspires a hushed awe upon entering in.

Tears welled up and spilled silently over the dam of my lower lid as I pulled out a fresh page and began to write—the first of so many poems I would write in, about, and because of this space.

How did I come to be here on that enchanted evening late in May 2009? It was two days after my birthday and coming to open mic was how I wanted to celebrate. Yet that's not the beginning. I could say it started one dark, chilly December evening in 2006 when I picked up an early edition of *Always Running* by Luis J. Rodriguez while perusing the musty stacks in the second basement level of my graduate school library. But that's not really where this story starts either. I must go farther back.

I WAS 13 OR 14 YEARS OLD, engaged in a discussion with a teacher about what makes a person steal or do drugs. I remember stating, with indignation, that if people *really* wanted to, they could all just make the right decision. Every one has a choice after all. I could be confident in my position having been raised in an upper-middle-class Protestant Christian home. I, the blond-haired blue-eyed granddaughter of German immigrants, had plenty of opportunities to weigh options, because choices were always in abundance. My teacher ever so compassionately ended our conversation with the words, "No, people don't always have choices; not the same ones you and I have." It would be some years before I began to understand that the choices, and sheer number of them, I have are a privilege that came along with my fair skin.

In college I took courses in juvenile justice and tried to understand the dynamics and the particular circumstances that create a reality of kids stealing and slanging just to put food on the table for younger siblings. I researched gang intervention and outreach. I formulated curriculums and outlined programming. After college, I became a foster parent at a youth ranch so I could get inside part of the system and learn more about these beautiful children and youth who have been made castaways by the state. I learned how ill-equipped I was for serving these kids and realized I needed more training

so I could bring them better tools and resources. I understood that there were various ways to approach the idea of serving youth. My college courses in criminal justice inspired me to research becoming a probation officer, but my experience as a foster mother taught me that I wanted to connect with people independently from the system—I did not want to be bound to, restricted by, or associated with the system. I had found my answer. In the fall of 2006, I moved to California to complete my education and experience as a mental health counselor.

I continued seeking out ways to place myself alongside youth who were involved in gang-related activities, on probation, continually getting in fights, struggling in school, and getting frequent flier miles from numerous trips to the dean's office. I saw so many times that behind the fierce exterior was a world of hurt, loss, trauma, and often times, abuse. Other times I saw kids who came from loving and supportive homes, yet who were more creative in their expression and thinking still struggled to fit in to the rigid structure of the system lacking outlets for their incredible artistry whether in performing skateboard tricks, in completing graff artworks, or in spitting wicked wit to beats spun by a DJ.

Because spaces like Tia Chucha's exist and thrive—despite all odds—artists like me are allowed to thrive. It is the welcoming, nurturing, empowering, and inspiring attitude of the community within Tia Chucha's that makes it possible for individuals of all ages to be known, and know others; to be validated as artists; to have a space to express and share that art; and to be transformed by the whole experience of doing art in community with others.

Aztec Goddess.
16x20 Acrylic and
Aerosol on Canvas,
2011. Artist:
Ramiro Alejandro
Hernandez (R@H), San
Fernando Valley artist.

When I picked up that copy of *Always Running* and read on the back cover how it was a story of a young man's experiences in "La Vida Loca," about how he got out, and began to give back to his community, I was sold. Several years after reading *Always Running* I was exploring books online and came across that author again, Luis J. Rodriguez. This time it was his book, *Hearts and Hands: Creating Community in Violent Times*, and from the description I was certain this book must have been tailor made for people like me. I tore into the volume the moment the box arrived at my door, but this would be no fast read like when I devoured *Always Running* in a matter of days. This would be a slow savoring read, with underlines and notes jotted in the margins, with exclamations and drawing parallels between ideas in the book and thoughts collected in my dream notebook. *Hearts and Hands* is where I first learned about Tia Chucha's and sat in awe and wonder that a place, so similar to what I had conjured in my imagination, actually existed right down the highway from me. There was no question—I must see the space in person and decided open mic night would be the perfect time for my first visit.

I never planned on reading that first night. I intended to slip quietly into some unnoticed back corner seat and just watch and soak it all up. I intended to remain anonymous; it always seemed safer that way. Yet despite all those intentions, I carried my notebook with me anyway. I had learned my lesson years before at the first open mic I ever attended, Sun Poet's Society in San Antonio, Texas. Once inside I found a table. I was a little embarrassed having been so overcome with emotion at seeing this tangible dream realized. Soon several people introduced themselves to me; they had just attended a workshop on the Aztec calendar and were staying for open mic. They asked if I would share anything that night and I shyly admitted that while I had some poems, I just came to watch. When the open mic emcee, Nery Boche, came around with the sign-up, my new acquaintances announced that I had poems and should be added to the list. The truth out, I felt there was no arguing at this point so I added my name to the others written there.

The lights darkened and I relaxed into the warmth of the space, but when I heard my name called, my heart was pounding and palms were sweaty. I regretted ever owning up to having any poems on me at all, wishing I could have just stayed unknown there in the back corner. I thought it had been a mistake, but my name was being called and my legs were walking me to the mic. I shared my pieces and immediately felt a flood of acceptance and embrace from the community. During the break and afterwards I shared words of appreciation with the other artists there, and they did so with me. Several people remarked how they were able to connect deeply with the words I had shared. Walls broke down across gender, age, ethnicity and we were there together, human beings, sharing our stories and art. I'm pretty sure I floated out to my car when the evening was over. Something quite magical had happened: I found community. I found home.

IN THE WEEKS AND MONTHS that followed, open mic at Tia Chucha's was my standing date on Fridays. I gushed giddy with excitement when late that summer Luis himself stopped in at open mic and I was able to meet him and tell him in person how much I appreciate his work and how I came to see him as a mentor, from the page, in my work with youth. I got to know the regulars that attended open mic each week and began to feel more comfortable on the mic. I also began to notice that there was a startling lack of women who would go up to the mic each week—there was a few of us, often the same two or three with an occasional visiting woman singer or poet. Many times at the break or afterwards women would approach me, share with me they have been writing for quite some time, but never shared any of their work out loud with anyone. I thought about the lack of women on the mic and about how women writers exist aplenty in this community and wondered how to bridge the two. After some conversations and scheming, I presented an idea for a women's writing circle to some of the staff, Stacy and Karina, who I had gotten to know while attending open mic. Their first reaction was, "Yes! We've been hoping someone would start something like that!" My first reaction was, "Oh no, I'm not going to start it; I'm not qualified. I just have the idea." I was encouraged to think about it and follow up with them. I wrestled with the idea very much wanting to empower the women I was meeting to share their songs, stories, and poems, yet I felt so inadequate never having taken a single writing course and not knowing anything to be able to teach. Yet somewhere within me I got the feeling that the last thing any of us wanted—myself included—was

Somewhere within me I got the feeling that the last thing any of us wanted—myself included—was someone to teach us how to write, but rather, very simply, someone to coax out the writer who was already within us yearning to bloom.

someone to teach us how to write, but rather, very simply, someone to coax out the writer who was already within us yearning to bloom. You see, I still had yet to call myself a writer. Oh sure, I wrote blogs, poems, and essays. But I wasn't a writer. No one had called me a writer. I wasn't published. Who was I to take on leading a writing circle?

Somehow I quieted that questioning voice and drafted a proposal for something called *In the Words of Womyn* (ITWOW) a writing circle workshop for women that would include a time for writing, for learning about published women writers, and for sharing our own work. I decided that the mission of ITWOW would be simply, "to give sound to our story and volume to our voice," and that we would accomplish this through the practice and performance of written and spoken-word. I submitted my proposal to the staff and

ITWOW 2010.
Tia Chucha's.
Symlar, CA.
Photo:
Luz Rodriguez

In the Words of Womyn workshop began on January 15, 2010. As of December 2011, ITWOW has completed six 10-week workshop sessions. These sessions connected with over 75 women in Northeast San Fernando Valley and the greater Los Angeles County. They have created opportunities for women to perform at such events as Tia Chucha's annual anniversary event and Celebrating Words Festival. Many cheered as the women performed on the mic for the first time. We have also published over 100 poems, stories, and essays online at www.inthewordsofwomyn.com. And we've celebrated with the numerous women who have begun to call themselves writers.

BECAUSE SPACES LIKE TIA CHUCHA'S exist and thrive—despite all odds—artists like me are allowed to thrive. It is the welcoming, nurturing, empowering, and inspiring attitude of the community within Tia Chucha's that makes it possible for individuals of all ages to be known, and know others; to be validated as artists; to have a space to express and share that art; and to be transformed by the whole experience of doing art in community with others. The individual transformation spills over into community transformation, as youth find a place where they are accepted, embraced, and allowed to express freely; as women find their voices and turn up the volume; as elders are given the space to share wisdom and stories; and where all people can cultivate their identities and inspire one another as they create and share together.

Tia Chucha's isn't just about the four walls. Tia Chucha's is about a vision, about the passionate living out of art and minds meeting for change, about people of all different ages, religions, orientations, political beliefs, skin colors, languages, and experiences finding family among one another—about a community being transformed.

My
Dream

BY MARIA MORALES

I chose pen and paper over pots and pans.

I said, "No" to the old traditions of listen and obey.

I went to school against my mother's wishes. She wanted an obedient daughter to teach to be just like her, a perfect mother and wife. But I went to school and listened to my teachers instead.

They filled my head with dreams of becoming a teacher just like them. My teachers told me that I could conquer the world because my place was the entire world, not only the four walls of home.

I fought a war at home because I was different. I wanted to learn the written word. I wanted to write my own stories. My parents let me go to another country. In there, I found the freedom that I always longed for. Nobody put me down anymore. I was free to read and write. My hands get tired of writing, but my heart is always singing a song about my fulfilled dream.

On
Inspiration

BY LALOW

Where does inspiration come from?
Well, it's in the word: Spirit.
Our infinite nature.
Timeless.
Without beginning or end.
Clothed in our flesh.
Cloaked in secrecy.

Can you hear it when it calls you?
Do you acknowledge it when it shows up in your life?

In a homeless person, reminiscing with a smile
    on her face.
In a child, angry that he feels out of place,
Still clinging to the knowledge that there is more
    to this life
Than what we see with our physical eye.
We do our best to make sense of circumstances
That are ever changing.
And our Spirit remains present,
While we shift with a smile.

Can you sense it in your breath?
That invisible force that sustains our life.
That unconscious process of exchange that connects
Our heart to our mind.
Our rhythm.
That connects us to one another.
Our true nature.
Permanent in a world of impermanence.
A seeming contradiction, but, then again,
Words are only clothing for our thoughts,
Which veil the secret that can be heard anywhere
When we listen in stillness.

I know you have heard it.
For I have seen it.
In a homeless person with a smile on her face,
Drunk from the spirits.
In a child filled with anger,
Raging with an energy that seeks to strike out against
Something he has been taught to perceive as
   different than himself;
If only to connect with another for a fleeting moment.

I know you have felt it.
But can you recognize it in others?
How do you acknowledge it when it shows up
   in your life?

Untitled

By Michael Dwyer

I've witnessed the kindness a stranger can give,
without judgment or thought, but a love just to give.
A benevolent moment no matter the length,
to give without question, shows volumes of strength.
It saddens the elders and ancients that see,
how we stumble and clamber so desperate to be,
something quite grabbing for we strive and we try,
we run round and round in circles, though we don't
   know the why.
We're riddled with promises that tell us of ease,
but only with sacrifice, 'til you've tendered your fees.
Take what is heard and simply thought of to be,
discard it with courtesy, give it up to the breeze.
You'll find what was once so joyously kept,
in the soul of a man 'til he parted with death.
These days we're maniacal we forget why we're here,
deep down on the inside we all wish to see clear.
I promise you kin, my brothers that are,
to find what you seek, you needn't look far.
For you see you're bestowed with such wonderful sight,
you were born and forgot that you were bred
   from the light.
And although the confusion had set you apart,
you can finally see, the key was kept in your heart.
So anointed ones please, won't you take for the trees,
there is much to be done, with your soul to appease.
We all take a path that is unique for our stay,
your body a vessel, as your soul guides the way.
It will make for a journey as smooth as a dream,
this life is miraculous, scores more than is seen.
I long for the day when I can breathe out a sigh,
and let go of this land and sail through the sky.
'Til then I enjoy my part in this play,
I can't help but smile as I float through my days.

Meso-American Studies | Acquiring Pre-Hispanic Thought and Culture to Heal and Transform

BY COZKACUAUHTLI HUITZILZENTEOTL

I WAS TWELVE YEARS OLD when we moved to Pacoima from Barrio Van Nuys. I arrived with a certain degree of street knowledge, typical in children raised in broken homes and in neighborhoods characterized by poverty and its symptoms: alcohol, drugs, gangs, and violence. Although the demographics in Pacoima differed from the demographics of Van Nuys, my barrio know-how was transferable. I respected others. I didn't snitch. I minded my own, and I held my ground.

In the early 1980s, Mexicans and Mexican-Americans were present in Pacoima, yet outnumbered by African-Americans. At this time there were Mexican and Chicano gangs, Black gangs, and hybrid gangs composed of Mexican, Chicano, and Black youth. The latter grouping was most evident at the high school level.

By age 17, I became part of the norm. I was affiliated with gangs—drinking, getting "high," and having unprotected sex. As a result, I soon dropped out of high school and was facing parenthood. Because of immaturity and unpreparedness, my relationship ended shortly after my son's birth. Two years later, I had a daughter with another woman. I was frowned upon, even by my loved ones. I recall asking myself, "*¿Qué le pasa a mi familia?* / What's wrong with my family?" It seemed as if we were cursed. My mother was the only one in my family who had finished high school and university. Those of my generation, my *primos* (cousins) and I, were even worse off than our parents who had migrated to the United States. It's almost as if my mother's victories as a single parent had gone unnoticed, because just like my *primos* and friends, I too strolled diligently down the grim path to self-destruction.

Aztec Street. Sylmar, CA. Photo: Javier Martinez

ALL ALONG, hip-hop was part of my life. I expressed myself artistically and emotionally mostly through popping and rhyming. I studied raps by KRS One, Chuck D, Paris, X-Clan, and others of the sort. In fact, my first history mentors were conscious rappers. Their lessons prompted me to question many things, such as, "How can we break away from the vicious cycle that mangles us?" I soon realized that the African-American experience was sim-

> **Learning history from the indigenous perspective helps extract narratives that contrast the views propagated by the first European invaders and western academe.**

Meso-American books. Tia Chucha's. Sylmar, CA. Photo: Javier Martinez

ilar to mine; our peoples shared unsuccessfulness.

Eventually, I launched an identity quest and thus ended up checking out an array of books on the Native Peoples of the Caribbean and the Americas from a public library. In a short period of time, I read every single one, which was a major accomplishment for me. Interestingly enough, something happened to me while in the process. I began to piece together my own historical narrative. I started to understand where my people stood in today's society and why we were in such dire conditions. It was cause and effect.

On one hand, I read about European invasions, the colonization of native peoples, genocides, land annexations, and the systematic breakdown of my ancestors. On the other hand, I learned of the advanced civilizations created by various indigenous groups throughout Mexico and Central America. I now appreciated my ancestry at a new level. I began to respect myself, yet a feeling of hurt still tingled within. I disliked the fact that my people had been hustled by invaders—the Spanish and more recently the Anglo-Americans.

At first, the rage that came from becoming aware served as the impetus that propelled me into Los Angeles Mission College. Later in life, it was a sense of obligation to my people, the oppressed, that motivated me to reach California State University of Northridge, where I obtained my Bachelors in Liberal Arts, a teaching credential, and a Master of Arts in Education. From this experience I learned that it's not until one analyzes history from a stance relevant to their own existence, that one can strategically forge a plan to surpass the obstacles before them.

In the 1980s through 1990s, Pacoima parks were mostly used as drug dispensaries and gang recruiting grounds. Our community offered no cultural centers, no bookstores, nor other creative outlets to stimulate and evolve the mind. If something existed, it sure wasn't evident.

Fortunately, Mission College provided me what my barrio hadn't. It became a place of enlightenment. I learned to network with others who were also on the path to self-awareness and political activism. At Mission, I took my first Chicano Studies classes, which immediately captivated me. Studying my people's history, struggles, victories, literature, and testimonies broadened my cultural and historical peripheries. For the first time in my life, school was relevant and thus meaningful to me.

A new level of awareness developed at Mission College and it awoke in me the need to see, firsthand, the cultural wealth of my ancestors. I began to travel to Mexico to visit some of its many archeological sites. The first ancient city that I visited was Teotihuacán. The experience was beyond words. I was in awe. I felt that if other barrio youth could experience the grandeur of their ancestors, then perhaps they too could begin to heal as I had. At Mission I met Meztli, a nurse of Mixtec descent, who was raised in Mexico City. We had many things in common. We had been teenage parents, loved our ancestral culture, and were both interested in the ongoing indigenous struggles throughout America. After our first date, we never parted from each other. I now had a revolutionary companion!

It was through college that I got connected with danzantes, Aztec dancers—an experience that further added to my indigenous identity. My thirst for ancestral knowledge and my experience as a break dancer allowed me to learn dances at a quick pace. Even though most dancers attempted to preserve the dances to the best of their abilities, it wasn't long before I realized that most of the dancers were ignorant to their "true" history. They seemed to be comfortable with mixing native traditions with Catholicism, but I felt something was wrong. I believed that the dances and ceremonies we inherited from our ancestors should be respected and preserved. This is something that I addressed later in life.

Meanwhile, Meztli and I engaged in yearly trips to Mexico and Central America to study the Zapatista revolt and other contemporary indigenous struggles. We witnessed extreme levels of poverty throughout Mexico and the negative effects of low-intensity wars against native peoples and their sympathizers. The communities that were occupied by military bases reminded me of home. They were dilapidated, full of misguided youth, drugs, alcohol abuse, violence, and prostitution. On the other hand, in liberated Zapatista territories, such ills were less evident. In Chiapas I experienced what a mobilized and organized community looked like. I recall learning about the Jewish holocaust in school, but never about the Native American holocaust. The murdering and displacing of indigenous people throughout America has not only occurred in history, it's ever-present and ongoing.

On one occasion, while deep in the jungles of Chiapas, Meztli and I asked Comandante Tacho how we could be of assistance in the effort to liberate indigenous people and he responded, "Organize yourselves!

It's not until we're able to see life and its occurrences though our own cultural-historical lens, that we can truly understand our peoples' accomplishments and struggles.

Mexicans and Chicanos living on the other side of the border need to organize their communities, so that together we can create a better world." He left me thinking, "Before we can build a movement of solidarity with others, we must first be engaged in a local movement of change and liberation."

In 1997, the Los Angeles Indigenous Peoples' Alliance (LAIPA) invited lecturers from the Nahuatl University (Universidad Náhuatl), situated in Ocotepec, Morelos, Mexico, to present at Ritchie Valens Park in Pacoima. The keynote speakers, Mariano Leyva and Martha Ramirez Oropeza, held seminars on pre-Hispanic history, calendars, languages, philosophies, and sciences. They challenged western academe and assisted us in understanding and developing our indigenous perspective.

They emphasized the importance of recovering our original roots and outlook to live a more dignified and meaningful life. Their workshops were intriguing! On a few occasions we met with Maestro Arturo Meza in Malinalco and in Mexico City to learn more about, indigenous history, language, codices, and calendars. We learned so much that we no longer were the same. As advised by the Maestros (teachers), we set out to disseminate all the information that we had acquired.

El indigenismo, nativism, was the missing element. All along, my danzante comrades, Chicano Studies professors, and I had accepted the "official" version of history without questioning much of it. The official version of history is not designed to teach us that we're descendants of the original peoples of America, because that would be empowering. Instead, we're taught to embrace identities or terms such as Hispanic—when most of us would find it impossible to track a living relative in Spain. The denial of our native self can be partly attributed to the Eurocentric viewpoints instilled in us in educational and religious institutions. We've been conditioned to feel disinterest, shame, and abhorrence towards our indigenous self, a crucial part of our existence, the part that, if developed, can keep us focused and grounded throughout life.

RECONNECTING WITH THE VAST knowledge of our ancestors can be our exit ticket from the self-destructing cycle we're caught in. Oppressed people need to heal from their historical traumas in order to break away from what Dr. Joy Degruy calls Post-Traumatic Slave Syndrome (PTSS), which describes "the negative behaviors and inferior self-images common in colonized persons due to multigenerational oppression." I was convinced that the rebirth of our original culture and thought needed to be part of the solution in transforming our lives and community.

The *Mexihcah*, Aztecs, of central Mexico used the phrase *In Ixtli In Yollotl* (literal interpretation: The Face, The Heart) as a general way to describe the human. Professor Fermin Herrera from California State University, Northridge (CSUN) affirms that the *"yollotl"* is a person's brute or "raw" nature. He teaches that the *"ixtli"* represents the building of "face," which involves becoming skilled and refined. Consequently, *In Ixtli In Yollotl* describes our human need to balance our raw potential with disciplines that will aid us in developing into civilized and virtuous citizens. It's for this reason that ancient leaders were often buried wearing beautiful and elaborate jade or turquoise masks—as a means to communicate their exemplary role or "face" in society.

Since the Europeans colonized the Americas, a major problem in our communities, particularly with the youth, has been the loss of identity and the misuse of our potential or "heart." This void of identity and purpose leads to self-hate and destruction. The studying of *Anahuac* accomplishments and history serves as a means to discipline ourselves in order to promote pro-

Sixth Sun. 9x14 Acrylic on Canvas, 2011. Artist: Ramiro Alejandro Hernandez (R@H). San Fernando Valley artist.

gressive changes in our lives and environment. In 1998, a handful of persons formed a native dance group called *Tloqueh Nahuaqueh*, which in *Nahuatl* means, "that which is close and together." We decided to teach pre-Hispanic dance, music, history, traditions, and sciences at Hubert Humphrey Park in Pacoima. Within the first two years, we developed study groups, councils for women, children, men, musicians, dancers, and vendors. As a means to govern ourselves, we implemented an indigenous method and philosophy known as the *Calpulli* system. We started utilizing our culture to organize, educate, heal, express, honor, celebrate, and in some cases to supplement our income—by selling our foods, crafts, textiles, and other native goods. Some of us met to create Meso-American curriculum, lessons, and workshops. In addition, we further studied Nahuatl with Professor Fermin Herrera to better prepare ourselves. The *Anahuac* rebirth was underway!

Meztli and I organized annual Mexico trips with Chicano youth to better expose them to their culture. Through time, many of the young men and women voluntarily stopped gang-banging, some changed their behavior and their way of dressing. Others used their *cultura* (culture) as a source of inspiration that became evident in their artistic creations. Marginalized women of low self-esteem now had a voice in their homes and therefore took a more active role in guiding their family towards a healthier lifestyle. It became apparent that many participants changed significantly. Individuals that partook in the process at one point or another now carried themselves with a new sense of self-respect, dignity, and purpose.

MEXIHCAYOTL 101

TÍA CHUCHA'S Cultural Café and Bookstore opened its doors at the end of 2001 and immediately became the cultural sanctuary of the Northeast San Fernando Valley. In no time, the center was hosting classes, workshops, and events involving all art forms. Tia Chucha's quickly became a regional resource that involved stu-dents of all ages, artists, activists and families from surrounding communities. It was 2009 when I formally joined the Tia Chucha's family. I started collaborating with Ome Acatl, who had started a class titled *Mexih-cayotl 101*. In *Nahuatl, Mexihcayotl* literally means "Mexicanness," but the term is widely used to describe the study of indigenous culture and history. Ome and I designed and delivered lessons on diverse aspects of Meso-American civilizations. In addition, we incorporated a *Nahuatl* component into every study session. In

The thundering of the Aztec drums and the enchanting Nahuatl songs seem to activate spectators' subconscious minds—allowing them to feel a natural calling and attraction.

a short matter of time, our class grew. Later, due to some circumstances of life, I ended up as the Mexih-cayotl facilitator. I continued teaching on native thought, sciences, and traditions.

The *Mexihcayotl* classes taking place at Tia Chucha's are part of an ongoing collective effort to transform our communities through the diffusion of our ancestral culture. Since native peoples have been broken-down or degenerated systematically, a counter program was necessary—one that consistently empowers marginalized persons. Tia Chucha's leadership and staff have been essential in supporting our attempt to disseminate the cultura. Not only do we teach and hold workshops at the centro, its staff in turn networks with other agencies to help broaden our audience. The centro also creates job opportunities that help take our workshops offsite to the larger community.

As a result, a comprehensive and practical *Anahuac* studies program is being implemented in the Northeast San Fernando Valley with the intent to heal and transform our barrios. The program entails a rigorous study of indigenous peoples' histories, languages, sciences, and arts. All of which are offered by mitotiqueh, Aztec dancers, at Tia Chucha's and local community parks. There are an increasing number of residents of the Northeast Valley that can attest to the effectiveness of the Mexihcayotl classes. Studying indigenous history has helped many validate their existence and hence understand their actual reality.

Through this discipline, many have linked their families to specific geographical regions of Meso-America and therefore the languages, traditions, and oral histories of the area. Furthermore, learning history from

Our ancestors used the arts, including painting and sculpturing, as a means to preserve and relay knowledge, legends, and stories from one generation to the next.

the indigenous perspective helps extract narratives that contrast the views propagated by the first European invaders and western academe. It's not until we're able to see life and its occurrences though our own cultural-historical lens, that we can truly understand our peoples' accomplishments and struggles. By analyzing history through our own perspective, we can identify some of the root causes to our self-hating attitudes and behaviors. The personal enlightenment that comes from studying relevant history often evolves into some sort of community activism for social change.

THE STUDY OF NAHUATL has also been crucial in developing our identity and in furthering our studies on Meso-American civilizations. It provides Nahuatl enthusiasts the etymological knowledge needed to extract the meaning of Nahuatl terms or phrases featured in history texts and documentaries. This is important because historians more than often offer erroneous and academically irresponsible interpretations. For example, in "official" versions of history the words Coatl Icue are often interpreted as "The Earth Monster," when in fact they mean "She of Serpent Skirt." Most historians mis-

interpret the word Quetzalcoatl and write that it means "feathered serpent" when it should read "precious serpent" (quetzal means "precious," not "feather").

The acquiring of the Nahuatl language also allows us to savor the Mexican and Central American variances of Spanish. For example, taco, mole, and guacamole are some of the nearly five-hundred words in the Spanish language that derive from Nahuatl. Because language is such an intricate aspect of culture, learning Nahuatl is yet another way to preserve our indigenous heritage and identity. An ongoing study of Nahuatl results in the learning of a distinct thought process that enables students to begin to comprehend their ancestors' literature and cosmo-vision.

Examining the scientific implementations of Meso-America promotes scientific thinking and assists individuals in coming to terms with nature and the cosmos. For example, there's power in learning that the ancient peoples of Mexico and Central America developed their own writing and number systems, a feat only shared by four other ancient world cultures. This realization allows individuals to see their ancestors as scientists and not as superstitious or religious fanatics as often interpreted in official texts. For example, it's been engrained in us that the Aztecs sacrificed people to ensure that the sun would rise, when in fact they had pyramids (tzcualli) marking exactly where the sun would rise on particular dates: solstices, equinoxes, zeniths, etc. If we take into account the thousands of ancient native cities that are astronomically aligned, it becomes apparent that our ancestors didn't leave anything to chance or faith—it was all pre-calculated.

Furthermore, the manner in which our ancestors organized time is also part of our grand cultural heritage. The unique design, organization, mechanics, and precision of Meso-American calendars further prove the sophistication of our predecessors. The learning and using of such calendar systems makes persons aware of their environment. Pre-Cuauhtémoc calendars did more than just keep track of the days—they were synchronized with natural cycles, such as, the flora and fauna. Moreover, astronomical occurrences (e.g., solstices, equinoxes, and zeniths) were also correlated with particular day-glyphs and months. An extraordinary result that comes from using original peoples' calendars is that it transforms ordinary persons into Earth scientists and naked-eye astronomers. Incidentally, individuals who use natural calendars, like the "Aztec," learn to ground themselves to the earth and universe, which serves as a form of relief from the mechanical routine associated with the Gregorian calendar that governs us today.

Following the tradition of our ancestors, there are an increasing number of persons who have used native calendars to name their children. Also, many adults now identify more so with their indigenous calendar name, than with their colonial birth name. Some have gone as far as to change their name legally.

OF THE MESO-AMERICAN studies program, the arts are perhaps the most engaging to the community. The thundering of the Aztec drums and the enchanting Nahuatl songs seem to activate spectators' subconscious minds—allowing them to feel a natural calling and attraction. For the practitioner or mitotiqui, it's the combination of ancestral music, songs, and dances that becomes the vehicle through which one best harmonizes with the environment. Hence, the arts have a soothing and healing effect on both, the spectator and the presenter.

Pre-Hispanic performing arts convey Meso-American cosmo-visions and sciences. Our ancestors used the arts, including painting and sculpturing, as a means to preserve and relay knowledge, legends, and stories from one generation to the next. For example, the name, theme, and movements of each dance always transmit indigenous knowledge of natural and astronomical phenomena. In this sense, the mitotiqui becomes an animated or virtual codex, whose function is to express and document the movements of life and of celestial bodies: the sun, moon, planets, etc. The feeling of wellness and connectedness that comes from "knowing," singing and dancing is often described by mitotiqueh (dancers) as their "spirituality."

Long ago, the arts were an essential part of Meso-

The Prophecy. 24x48 Oil on wood, 2010.
Artist: Rick Ortega. San Fernando, CA.

American society. For example, the Mexihcah (Aztecs) developed their artistic skills in public schools (nemachtiloyan) and in performing arts centers (cuica-calli). At that time, women, men, children, and elders all partook in monthly civic and agricultural ceremonies that featured music and dance.

Today, the arts are an essential part of our indigenous resistance. On one hand, we replicate our ancestors' work in order to help maintain and promote it. On the other hand, we draw inspiration from their accomplishments to create innovative contemporary works of art. Many of us channel our ancestors through the arts, and thus, honor and invite them to our cultural celebrations, marches, protests, and so forth. By far, the arts serve as the major entry way to the amazing world of our ancestors.

INDIVIDUALS WHO EMBARK on the task of learning any one of the Mexihcayotl components—relevant history, Native American languages, pre-invasion sciences, and original peoples' arts—tend to experience a new level of self-awareness and a certain degree of refinement. Those who are able to gradually study all of the components delineated above, for the most part, become distinguished stakeholders in the effort to promote personal and social change.

Transformation is a cumbersome task. It takes time and dedication, but more importantly, it takes convincing. As an educator I've learned that regardless of age, humans change and evolve when their learning is assisted and guided. Individuals are willing to master "new" skills and concepts that are relevant to their existence. In addition, the learning process is more effective when it includes teacher scaffolding and provides opportunities for self-discovery. For such reasons, the Mexihcayotl program has resulted effective in developing cultural-historical awareness and thus promoting progressive change.

In the Nahuatl language the word *tlamatini* means the same as "scientist." It describes "One who habitually knows things." Mexihcayotl participants that have attended consistently have demonstrated significant change. Their historical outlook, demeanor, and conversation have become more sophisticated. Most regulars have developed into analytical historians— equipped with primary sources and the indigenous perspective. While some persons in the Northeast Valley negate or grapple with their identity, others are actively engaged in becoming cultural-historical mentors or *tlamatinimeh* ("sages")

Etymology of the word tlamatinimeh:

tla + mati + nimeh

3. things + 2. know + 1. ones who habitually…

Tlamatini**meh** is the plural form of tlamatini. Nahuatl word parts are read as such: From suffix to verb to prefix (from rear to front).

If We Could, We Would

By Harold Terezón

build vocational centers
to educate without prejudice
of illiteracy, experience,
status, language, or color

have fearless educators
teach at our new library,
schools, the gardens,
the church, Ritchie Valens Park

conjure la siguanaba,
cucuy, & la llorona
in vibrant murals
to put the fear back
in the hearts that destroy

reprogram old ways
of thinking that nature,
magic, city, imaginary maids
will clean up after us

clone more Luis J. Rodriguez'
to have on every corner
of every block praising love
of music, art, & poetry

require Univision, KNBC,
KABC, KTTV, KCAL,
& Telemundo to air
a segment of love
& determination
for every segment
of violence & drugs
they already air

march in masses
to the chemical plants,
tear them down, detoxify
& build parks our kids
could breathe & play in

rebuild the streets
teach our local history
reclaim our streams,
canyons, & rivers,
desert, & sky,
dreams, & voices

resurrect Huggy Boy &
usher in Art Laboe
to broadcast the love
that drives inside us

Practice

By Jeffrey Martin

No matter my appearance
you will find me
a tough nut to crack

I do bend and tremble
under the heat
but never break

Your position above me
will never turn me
passive
or give enough reasons
to change what I like
about myself

If you take it upon
yourself
to speak to the universe
on my behalf
she will tell you
subtly
that she has given up
trying to reduce me
to ashes
for she knows all too
well
that I am willing to die
rather than
demote my life
to that which finds
itself in trash receptacles

My battle scars
are quite heavy
at times
but the metamorphosis
granted through those
lessons
enhance my endurance
and give me small pockets
of joy
as reminders of what
those like you
want to take away

I will not apologize
for a resilience
made of driftwood
cast to and fro
strengthened by
the very waves
wanting its demise

The birds of prey
having hovered above
my exposed soul
grew frustrated
stating my taste bitter
unworthy of their palates
but truth be told
the meaty substance
between my ears
was not ready to be
consumed
for it was just beginning
to hone and expand itself

Untitled

By Angie Sea

Math, Science, and Technology
Everything is so different from how it used to be
No more factory workers on the assembly line
Just machines and belt lines
Jobs are overseas so stand in the unemployment line
This country is losing its mind
What ever happened to "No child left behind?"
1 minute to read this
3 minutes to comprehend that
Test after test
Leaves the child in distress
It doesn't help that the teacher is a mess
Teaching in fear that at the beginning of his/her career the end of it is so near
With Budget cuts and constant layoffs, no class room supplies
All their books do is teach our children lies
We're 38th in education in the world
Chasing the coat tails of France, China, Australia and the other 34 I won't mention
Their children are interested in numbers, and ours need intervention
With no family connection and lack of education
Our children turn to the streets and listen to the media
With Reality TV stars as their role models
Believing that Hollywood is glamorous
The world isn't what it seems
Everyone lives beyond their means
Living their lives on credit
We need a cure for this disease of individualism and materialism
Obsessed with celebrities that live their lives at ease
While your mom is scrubbing their floor on her knees
Begging you please, "Go to School, don't be a fool and become another statistic"
Like Luis Rodriguez, I'm "Always Running"
Toward a better tomorrow
So our youth don't have to live in sorrow
Held down my society
Living in constant anxiety that there is nothing left for them to look forward too
With the help of community organizations, you, and me
We can cure the youth
With writing, art, music, and unity
And with Mayra and the Young Warriors leading the way
The youth are headed for much better days.

The Young
Warriors.
February 2012.
Sylmar, CA.
Photo:
Estevan Oriol

Young Warriors | Every Youth is a Warrior of Their Own Struggles

MAYRA ZARAGOZA, FOUNDER
AS TOLD TO DENISE M. SANDOVAL

Young Warriors is a "for youth by youth" program created to provide meaningful and educational workshops and events to the youth of the Northeast San Fernando Valley. Young Warriors offers a series of self-development workshops to assist youth in building their self-esteem as well as their communication skills through music, culture and the arts in order to bring out the gifts the youth carry within. This will allow them to pursue their callings in life and enable them to use their callings to guide them to learn self-discipline.

WHAT MOTIVATED ME to start Young Warriors was when I was fifteen I became politically aware of what was going on in the community, including all the injustices. I was a 10th grade student at San Fernando High School. Trini and Luis saw me at community meetings. They approached me to see if I was serious about starting my own youth center, something I mentioned at those meetings. Growing up in Pacoima—you don't always notice it but then you have it pointed out to you—there are many billboards promoting alcohol. You go to nicer neighborhoods and they don't have them. You go down the street here and you have a liquor store on every corner; you go to a nicer neighborhood and you have more markets than liquor stores. Pacoima has one of the biggest landfills, which some people are not aware of. These are things that we should not accept. We should want more and deserve more. We don't deserve to feel like we live in a community that has been forgotten.

If no one was going to help the youth, I thought it was up to me to do something. In 2007 I officially created Young Warriors. I was sixteen. I started having weekly meetings, although every week was different. We had youth dialogues and we showed documentaries to get participants to be more politically and culturally aware. We had a week on the arts and the youth could create anything they wanted. During that week, meetings started at 5 pm and would last until 8 pm because the youth were creating art and they didn't want to stop. At the beginning about seven to ten people participated. We met at the Pacoima Community Center. Little by little the center placed limits on our time, so we needed a new space to meet. I recruited students from my high school, as well as Vaughn Middle School/High School and Discovery Prep High School. The youth liked the dialogues and they were given a safe space to express themselves. They wanted this to be more than just one day a week. Unfortunately, I was a full- time high school student and unable to do this more than once a week.

AT FIRST MY WHOLE IDEA was to just have a youth center. One time I had a meeting with the youth and asked them what kind of center they wanted. One of them said a 24-hour youth center. That is one of my goals—to one day have a 24 hour-youth center. One of the reasons expressed about a center was because at times youth don't want to go home. Some youth have suicidal thoughts. Or

they want a place safe and fun to go to. Students are falling through the cracks because there are teachers in this community that do not care about the youth. I've had youth tell me that teachers won't allow them in class because of the way they look. Some teachers feel threatened by them. In my opinion, if a teacher is feeling threatened they should not be teaching in this barrio— they should go teach somewhere else. This creates a big issue with authority, and this makes it difficult for youth to trust adults or want to learn.

Tia Chucha's changed my life because they gave me the opportunity to turn my dream into a reality. If it weren't for them, I would not be where I am today. Issues the community is facing include the school-to-prison pipeline, gangs, and environmental injustice. The youth are facing concerns about their self-identity

Young Warriors made me realize that I'm more important than I thought I was. Every day I wake up thinking of making positive changes in the community...

—Juan Alzaga

Juan Alzaga
Photo: Estevan Oriol

Young Warriors brings youth together, and helps us find what we want to do in life to reach our full potential.

—Violet Soto

and what to do with themselves. There are not a lot of resources for people, especially youth, in the community. There are no theaters, bookstores, or big shopping malls like there are on the other side of the San Fernando Valley. Tia Chucha's provides that space of belonging and comfort for people. It educates people through their programming. They provide healing through the arts as well as in other areas. It never occurred to me to align my mind, body and soul. This is very important—and coming to spaces like Tia Chucha's is very powerful.

My goal for creating Young Warriors is to help the youth find what interests them and get them involved with community. I want to provide the opportunity and space where youth can became aware of the injustices going on around them—for them to want to improve themselves as well as their community.

Today Young Warriors is giving the youth skills they need to succeed in life such as leadership, critical thinking, communications skills, focus, and motivation. Our current project involves "Community Mapping" where we are creating a map highlighting small businesses that people should financially support, as wells as mapping "unhealthy areas" in those neighborhoods, like landfills/toxic sites, liquor stores, billboards and fast food chains. We are working toward informing the community members of Pacoima and Sylmar regarding the importance of supporting small businesses and promoting community health/wellness. This project allows the youth to be engaged in the issues that their communities are facing, as well as create solutions. We believe if you give youth the knowledge and tools necessary to bring out the passion/gifts they carry within, they will become engaged and see a future for themselves. They will no longer be victims, but will overcome the struggles of life, learning from their own battles—because every youth is a warrior of their own struggles.

TOP: **Violet Soto**
LEFT: **Mayra Zaragoza**
RIGHT: **Jenni Lemus**
Photos: Estevan Oriol

Mayra brought me to Tia Chucha's and Young Warriors. I like that they help you to find yourself and they help you to find your talent…They always have a warm welcome and always show you respect. Groups like Young Warriors are important because youth need to learn to respect their community and help the community get better.

—Linda Hernandez

Mi Amor Para Mi Gente
(Excerpt)

BY MAYRA ZARAGOZA.

I am that *cihuatl*

That will capture

Your attention

With my

Intellectual

Political

Poetical words

That flow

Straight out of my corazón

As the love for my gente is real.

The passion

Embedded in my soul

Will have you

Feeling like

I have the answers

To solve

The mysteries

Of life….

Tia Chucha Press
A truly diverse and socially engaged small publisher

This is literature that matters, that makes a difference—that helps to positively define and shape the culture and times we're in.

FOR ALMOST TWENTY-FIVE YEARS, Tia Chucha Press has been known around the country as a quality small press of cross-cultural poetry collections. In 2012, TCP authors were featured in a special reading at the Associated Writers Program Conference in Chicago, the country's leading annual event for writers and teachers of writing.

A number of TCP authors have gone on to win a National Book Award, a Whiting Writers Fellowship, a Lannan Poetry Fellowship, National Poetry Slams, a Lila Wallace-Reader's Digest Writers Award, a Jackson Memorial Poetry Fellowship, and nominations for the Pulitzers and National Book Critics Circle Awards, among others. One of the poets, Elizabeth Alexander, published sixteen years before then, was chosen as 2009 inaugural poet for President Barack Obama.

The press began in Chicago by Luis J. Rodriguez with the 1989 publication of his first book, *Poems Across the Pavement*, which also won a Poetry Center Book Award from San Francisco State University. Designed by Jane Brunette of Menominee/French/German descent (who continues to design TCP books), this project opened the door to a new kind of publishing venture in the United States. An integral member of the thriving Chicago poetry scene—birthplace of the Poetry Slams in the mid-1980s—Luis was then approached by leading Chicago performance poets to do their first books (he also asked for manuscripts). Poets included Patricia Smith, David Hernandez, Michael Warr, Rohan B Preston, Jean Howard, Carlos Cumpian, Lisa Buscani, Tony Fitzpatrick, Dwight Okita and Cin Salach.

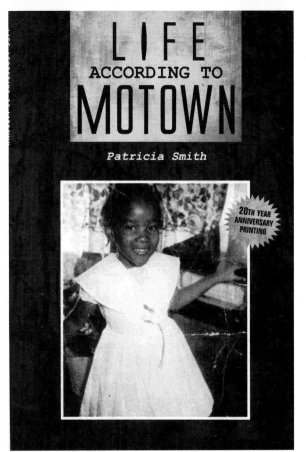

Tia Chucha Press books.

LEFT:
Dream of a Word: The Tia Chucha Press Poetry Anthology, 2006.

RIGHT:
Life According to Motown by Patricia Smith, 1991.

Soon, nationally-known writers sent in manuscripts and Tia Chucha Press published veteran poets such as Diane Glancy, Virgil Suarez, Nick Carbo, Kyoko Mori, Ricardo Sanchez, Melvin Dixon, and others. New writers of note over the years include Terrance Hayes, A. Van Jordan, Linda Rodriguez, Patricia Spears Jones, Linda Susan Jackson, Chiwan Choi, Susan D. Anderson, Jose Antonio Rodriguez, Richard Vargas, Luivette Resto, and Ariel Robello.

IN 1991, TIA CHUCHA PRESS became the publishing wing of the Guild Complex, a major non-profit literary arts presentation organization in Chicago (also co-founded by Luis), and later found a national distributor at Northwestern University Press. When Luis moved to the Northeast San Fernando Valley in the year 2000, he continued to select, edit, and publish books out of his home. Over the years, a volunteer editorial board assisted Luis, including Reginald Gibbons, Quraysh Ali Lansana, Julie Parson-Nesbitt, Mark Ingebretsen, and Mary Hawley. In 2005, with an agreement with the Guild Complex, Luis brought Tia Chucha Press from Chicago to become the publishing wing of the nonprofit Tia Chucha's Centro Cultural.

As of today, more than fifty perfect-bound individual collections have been beautifully designed and published as well as several anthologies, a CD, and chapbooks—from African Americans, Chicanos, Puerto Ricans, Cuban Americans, Japanese Americans, Native Americans, Korean Americans, Filipino Americans, Jamaican Americans, Irish Americans, Italian Americans... you name it.

This is literature that matters, that makes a difference—that helps to positively define and shape the culture and times we're in.

**Three Poems by
Tia Chucha Press poets:**

Architecture

By Chiwan Choi

i have taken to building in my sleep,
starting with small things—
a shelf for all my elephants,
four-feet wide and a foot deep,
with four legs six-inches tall,
a dining room table,
a new engine for my car.

today
i have built a mansion—
ten stories high,
stairs,
walkways,
bridges,
up and down and
sideways,
connecting everything to everything.

there are people in my architecture.
they walk in and out
of all the rooms.
i sit in the smallest room
with the comfortable green couch
as a woman tells me
of a song about a boat
that she used to listen to.
and holding my empty glass,
i tell her that i know that song
and sing out the lines about

the monkey taking his wife overboard.

i get up and walk to the bar,
turn back to see her cross her legs,
the left over the right,
smile
as she waves,
and i pour it full
with thick red wine
made with young grapes
and blood of bulls.

i take a sip
and walk out on a bridge,
look down at the house i have built,
the work of my hands
that remains beyond
comprehension.

(from 2010 THE FLOOD)

Painkiller

By Patricia Spears Jones

I can taste the metal
lose my desire for red meat

relax, every muscle
relax
emotion
relax
the time of day
I can give you
the time of day
What I talk about is how
love eludes me

No what I talk about is
what's wrong with me
No what I talk about is
what will happen to me

Fear
is the secret.
Always fear.

What you get from me is
the edge of a trace of shadows
and that's all you'll get
I can't give anymore
I don't want to
Everything hurts
painkiller interior

This hurtle into living space
and that swift slide out of it.

You want secrets
I say every reckless act
results from a moment of fear.
While compassion is the simple recognition

That what is done cannot be undone,
may not be forgiven.

And a recognition that the murderer and the martyr
the adulterer and the healer can at any moment
change positions, become the other.

It simply depends on how much pain
You need to kill.

(from 2010 PAINKILLER)

Freshman Class Schedule

BY JOSE ANTONIO RODRIGUEZ

I hate my freshman class schedule.
I'm in Algebra I, an advanced class
but not the most advanced,
which is where my friends are.

I'm stuck with idiots who don't understand
the relationships of angles.
It's all in the triangle, I want to scream
beneath my too-easy smile.

After the graduation ceremony,
my friends will walk away forever,
become engineers with expensive shoes,
sensibly-sized families. Even now
they are getting whiter every day.
Dreams of albino dollar bills
coat their pillows, I know it,

While I grow brown.
Brown like my father's forearms
which my freckle-faced mother insists
are only brown because of the years
bent over fields
Brown like the custodians
Brown like the Dairy Queen workers
Brown like the drop-outs
Brown like the juvies
Brown like the machos
Brown like the earthen floor
Brown like the outhouse
Brown like the soles of my feet when I run.

(from 2011 THE SHALLOW END OF SLEEP)

Acknowledgments

THIS BOOK AND RELATED FILM by John F. Cantu was made possible by a "Cultivate/Create" grant from the Los Angeles County Arts Commission. This grant was matched by donations made individually; online, including with an IndieGoGo campaign; at Tia Chucha events; and from talks made around the country. Part of another grant from the National Endowment for the Arts also went into the making of this book. Our thanks to the L.A. County Arts Commission for the training and orientation needed for Tia Chucha's to establish a new donor base.

Special thanks also to Tia Chucha's Cultivate/Create team of Dolores Villanueva, David Diaz, Ruben Guevara, and Walter P. Little for spearheading, coordinating, and insuring the success of this campaign. Thanks also to Trini Rodriguez and her staff for using inventive ways to bring in donations and for assisting with the culmination of the project. Thanks to Denise Sandoval and John F. Cantu for conducting the extensive interviews, gathering the materials, and spending hours upon hours in putting together this book and film. A special thanks to Estevan Oriol for contributing photography to this book, Jenuine for assisting with poetry submissions, Ramiro Hernandez for assisting with the art selections, Cornerstone Theater Company in Los Angeles, and Arte Público Press—University of Houston. Also thanks to Tia Chucha's board of directors during the time of this campaign: David R. Diaz, Dolores Villanueva, Mike de la Rocha, Carla Bykowski, Lee Ballinger, Wendy Carrillo, and Ron M. Daniels.

In addition, thanks to all the writers, artists, activists, musicians, dancers, instructors, organizers, and poets who contributed to this book. And thanks to board president Luis Rodriguez for taking this campaign wherever possible, raising funds and awareness, as well as co-editing this book.

THANKS, GRACIAS, TLAZHOKAMATI TO ALL OUR DONORS:

$1,000 plus:
The Los Angeles County Arts Commission
National Endowment for the Arts
Matthew Cohen
Falcon Trading Company, Inc.
Richard and Shari Foos
Anonymous

$500-$999:
Jorge Garcia
Northern Arts and Cultural Centre
Tia Chucha's Open Mic Night
SA Studios Agency, LLC

$100-$499:
Lee Ballinger
Carla Bykowski
Alan Cohen
Ron Daniels
Mike de la Rocha
Guild Complex
Margo Halstead
Natalia Hernandez
The Herrera Family
Steve Jones
Walter P. Little
Margarita Lopez
Jeffrey Martin
Alex Reza
Dolores Villanueva-Harriman
Art Zapata
Tia Chucha's Mexicayotl Indigenous Cosmology workshop
Tia Chucha's In The Words of Womyn workshop
Luis J. Rodriguez's "It Calls You Back" readings at Tia Chucha's

And thanks to everyone who donated from $1 to $99—you all made this possible.

About the Editors

Denise M. Sandoval, Ph.D. is an Associate Professor of Chicana and Chicano Studies at California State University, Northridge and received her Ph.D. in Cultural Studies from Claremont Graduate University in 2003. She was the guest curator/community researcher for two exhibitions on lowrider culture at the Petersen Automotive Museum in Los Angeles: *La Vida Lowrider: Cruising the City of Angels (2007-08)* and *Arte y Estilo: The Chicano Lowriding Tradition* (2000), and has written various articles and essays for publication on the lowrider culture. Her research interests include popular culture, oral history, and Los Angeles history.

Luis J. Rodriguez is the author of poetry, children's literature, fiction, and nonfiction books, including the bestselling memoir, *Always Running, La Vida Loca, Gang Days in L.A.* He has spent more than thirty years speaking and reading in prisons, juvenile lockups, migrant camps, homeless shelters, Native American reservations, conferences, universities, colleges, festivals, public and private schools, and libraries throughout the United States as well as Mexico, Central and South America, Canada, Europe, and Japan. His latest book is *It Calls You Back: An Odyssey Through Love, Addiction, Revolutions, and Healing.*